# High Perfo Presentations

Public Speaking Tips
& Presentation Skills to
Engage, Persuade and Inspire!

Dee Clayton

First published in the United Kingdom in 2018

Copyright © Dee Clayton 2018

The moral right of the author has been asserted.

All rights reserved.

No part of this publication may be reproduced, stored in a retrieval system, or transmitted, in any form or by any means, without the prior permission in writing of the author, nor be otherwise circulated in any form of binding or cover other than that in which it is published, and without a similar condition including this condition being imposed on the subsequent purchaser.

ISBN 978-1-983-68403-6

Cover design by CuCo Creative

Illustrations by Tandem Design

www.SimplyAmazingTraining.co.uk

You know how senior managers want to achieve more and more every year so they can reach their true potential?

Well, at Simply Amazing Training, we work with executives and their teams to inspire high performance. We do that by:

Helping to eliminate any unwanted thoughts or behaviours.

Creating more productive mindsets, toolsets and skillsets.

Facilitating continual 'Aha Moments'.

We use unique approaches which we know are effective – just read our testimonials. And we are delighted to have 7 business awards under our belt so far; and at the time of publishing recently won silver in a national award and achieved finalist in four other national award categories.

Want to buy lots of these books? Amazing! We'd love to help – please contact us: info@SimplyAmazingTraining.co.uk.

## Praise for this book

We present all the time – sometimes without knowing it – so anything that enables you to master the techniques is key. Embracing the advice this **book** gives you could be the key to a more confident, captivating presentation.
**Kathryn Jacob OBE - CEO at Pearl & Dean**

I found the advice practical and effective. Using it in a recent regional operations review with US bosses – it benefitted me and my team because we were able to confidently and succinctly position our annual plans, leaving US visitors feeling confident and positive about the year ahead for the region.
**Marion Obergfell - Senior Director EMEA Marketing, Channel Strategy & Operations at Zebra Technologies Europe Ltd**

The importance and ability to shape your presentation to suit your audience is critical to your success. This book makes you reflect on what you have been doing with your presentations, and how you can enhance them to improve your performance and that of your teams. The book provides a structure to enable you to improve, and ensure you give your career the boost it needs.
**Jason Abbott - President at AmSafe Bridport Ltd**

People tell me I'm a confident presenter but that doesn't mean I can't improve. I found the SAS structure AMAZING! I apply it now to everything I do, lately I used it at an industry conference in London where I presented to 150 people. Following Dee's techniques enabled me to gain higher audience feedback scores and be invited back to speak again.
**Daniela Busseni - Head of Category Development at Premier Foods PLC**

I would suggest this book to 99% of you. As a European Sales person of +14 years I've attended many sales & presentations trainings, so I wasn't sure what else I could learn from Dee's approach. But I'm pleased to say I was very surprised how effective it has been. I enjoy very much, the confidence on stage that I've acquired, and I love to see that my audience is totally engaged/focussed on the topic I'm presenting.
**Matteo Barilla - European Key Account Manager, Scientific Channel at Kimberly-Clark S.r.l.**

Effective. Memorable presentations are those where the presenter engages their audience and draws them in by delivering their content with confidence and authority. This book provides a step-by-step guide on how to do just that and will change the way you think about giving presentations forever.
**Justine Perry - Managing Director at Cariad Marketing Ltd**

I've implemented some of the advice in these pages, specifically around Presenter Personality Styles to adapt my communication to those around me and I'm pleased to say it has led to better understanding, stronger working relationships, increased clarity and positive feedback. I'd highly recommend reading this book if you want to learn how to flex to your audience, improve teamwork, and get on in business.
**Dr Vinny Dhir - Senior Regional Sales Manager, Endoscopy at Boston Scientific Ltd**

So easy to read, and with great practical tips too. What a useful book! I've already identified my Presenter Personality Style and those of my team members. In reading through the book, I can immediately see where we'll gain some quick wins.
**Melanie Blyth - Global Marketing Manager at Shell UK PLC**

ABOUT THE AUTHOR

Prior to setting up Simply Amazing Training Ltd I worked on a wide range of products in different company settings. My experience took me from Jacob's Creek to Jammie Dodgers, Bernard Matthews to Boddingtons and Marigolds to Murphy's, developing expertise across many communication tools including TV, radio and cinema advertising, international event sponsorship and conferences. Now with 20+ years of management experience behind me and 10+ years of training professionals, I love enabling senior managers and their teams to improve performance.

I'm author of the book, 'Taming Your Public Speaking Monkeys – Building Confidence for Public Speaking and Presentations', a book for nervous presenters. This book aims to benefit all business professionals – even the really confident ones.

I use presentation skills as the vehicle to help professionals because it is so visible to the individual and to others. It is one of the only places you have to be you, with your unique strengths and weaknesses laid bare! That's why I love what I do – I get to work at a deeper level, with the natural, true you.

We enjoy working with clients who appreciate the value of investing in their people and themselves, who are committed to personal development and the continual improvement that drives performance. If you are open to new approaches and want to work together to change individual and/or team results, then read on!

ACKNOWLEDGEMENTS

Thank you to all my clients for sharing their highs and their lows with me and helping me to learn more every day; to my colleagues, suppliers and support network with special mention (in alphabetical order) to Alison, Andy, Anita, Claire, Dani, Debbie, Dom, Domi, Jason, Jennifer, Joe, Jon, Julie, Justine, Karen, Kathryn, Katie, Kerry, Lee, Skyler, Marion, Mary, Paul, and Rebecca. And finally, to my Simply Amazing Training Licensed Practitioners, present and future, who are passionate about sharing this message far and wide.

**Dedication**

To my family, especially my Mum and Dad, for all their unwavering love and support.

To Leon for his positivity and cups of tea as I shut myself away writing.

CONTENTS

Chapter 1 High Performance Presentations ................................ 1

Chapter 2 Presenter Personality Style ................................ 19

Chapter 3 The Relevance of Mindsets ................................ 39

Chapter 4 Low Performance Mindsets ................................ 45

Chapter 5 High Performance Mindsets ................................ 67

Chapter 6 Prepare for the Simply Amazing Structure™ (SAS) .. 89

Chapter 7 Create Your Simply Amazing Structure™ (SAS) ...... 107

Chapter 8 Final steps to completing the SAS, bringing it all together & audience interaction foundations ................................ 157

Chapter 9 Rapport – Working with the audience ................... 195

Chapter 10 Personal impact, presentation delivery and conveying information visually ................................ 211

Chapter 11 High Performance Presentations are interactive, interesting and inspiring ................................ 245

Chapter 12 Advanced techniques and a final word on High Performance Presentations ................................ 273

FOREWORD

Having met Dee several years ago, it was easy to see why she is so successful in her field, helping both individuals and teams alike including many of my friends and colleagues. As someone who has been fortunate enough to have travelled far and wide and been invited to give talks and presentations to groups ranging from a living room of a few people to arenas of thousands, I fully appreciate how challenging it can be to create and deliver an engaging, persuasive and inspiring talk, especially when time is limited.

Whether you are an individual wanting to climb the ladder, a manager looking to motivate your team or a CEO with a passion to inspire, Dee's insights into "Presenter Personality Styles" throughout the book will help. You will be able to more easily see your strengths, self diagnose your weaknesses and pin point where you may be missing key points altogether.

You'll see how to avoid the traps that many of us (including myself in the past!) have naturally fallen into, and learn Dee's "Simply Amazing Structure" (SAS) to prepare and deliver to your audience in a way that just makes sense, both to you delivering the message and to those who are listening and engaging...and once you have grasped and mastered the "SAS" you will be amazed at how quickly you can put together a captivating talk and deliver it in an engaging manner without the need to learn a word for word script or use an autocue. This section alone is priceless content.

"High Performance Presentations" will help, guide and teach

you how to give the best and perhaps most relaxed talks ever, helping you stand out from the crowd, impress those around you and achieve your goals whatever they may be.

How might you feel right now if the boss or organiser ran up to you and said "John is sick...we need you to take his place in 15 minutes!" Sound scary? Trust me when I say that this book could have you pushing to the front of the queue exclaiming "sure I can cover for John!"

As I said to Dee when I first read through this book "I struggle with my notes for talks as I don't do word for word, but I like a track to run on and this will solve all my problems. Not sure why I didn't think of it lol."

**Wes Linden - Amazon Best-Selling Author, Multi-Million Pound Business Leader, Direct Selling Hall of Fame Inductee, International Speaker and MC for world-renowned Mastermind Event.**

Meet Wes @ weslinden.com

# Chapter 1
# High Performance Presentations

## *Why are you interested in giving High Performance Presentations?*

As the name suggests, High Performance Presentations increase the effectiveness of your message, resulting in new opportunities, increased sales and a reduction in mistakes. They deliver easier, faster and better results and increase the chances of career enhancement for you and your team. And they create a high level of buy-in and strong levels of action. If you or your team want to engage, persuade and inspire more people with your talks, presentations and communications then read on!

Most people find that at some level, their presentations can improve. This book is designed to enhance your skills and awareness and take you to the point at which you can happily say you and your team deliver High Performance Presentations (HPPs) every time. The more you deliver HPPs the more you will grow, as will your brand, service, business or category and most likely your career.

You are probably already good in some areas of presenting (but don't worry if you aren't – this book will still help). But if you don't know *why* you are good, or you are unaware of the specific techniques you employ, how can you help those around you? Once you learn and employ these skills you'll be able to pass them on to others.

## Your best opportunity

Presentations are one of the best opportunities you and your team have to be noticed by those more senior or more influential – those who pull the strings in the approval of your project, the winning of a pitch, your next career move and so on. If you aren't yet delivering High Performance Presentations read on, change your ways and use your new skills to influence the board, clients or key stakeholders.

## How do you know if you deliver High Performance Presentations?

With the gift of hindsight, I'm aware that I haven't always delivered HPPs even though I considered myself a very good presenter – after all, that's what most people told me from a young age. From the time I entered a debating competition at school, talking about underage drinking (we went to the pub to celebrate our success!), to the time as Head Girl I spoke to full school assembly, my experiences of public speaking were all positive.

During my corporate career in food and drink marketing I'd frequently present new products or ideas and always got great feedback. I made an effort to make my presentations engaging by asking questions, and I themed them to make them interesting and even funny.

I presented on so many topics in so many places – on wine varietals in Australia, Pizza Hut PR in California, Murphy's in Cork and Jammie Dodgers in Wales. I've been an event conference presenter hundreds of times. I achieved bonuses, won some awards and was mostly content in my work.

I thought I was doing quite well. and I was doing well - but mostly compared to a 'low bar'.

## *The bar is low!*

In my opinion it's easy to be *seen* as a good presenter because the bar is so low. In most businesses the quality level of an acceptable presentation is shockingly low. You'll know this to be true if you've ever had to feign interest in a presentation whilst actually feeling uninspired. If you've done this once or more, you are adding to the issue.

## Most people haven't studied how to do it well

Unlike other areas in one's career, presenting is generally not studied, perhaps a day course here and there but not studied.

Most people don't know what makes a High Performance Presentation. They may have parts of it right, but very few people are taught how to give a presentation by someone who has spent their entire career learning from experts, observing others and aiming to continually improve their communications.

Generally, presentation skills are unconsciously learnt from your boss, or previous bosses, so just how good were they at presenting effectively? And if you and your boss are different Presenter Personality Styles (more on that in Chapter 2 and throughout the book) and you try to copy their style it's unlikely to work – you may come across as false.

If you are the boss, be aware that you are unwittingly teaching your team, and anyone who listens to you, what makes a good/acceptable presentation – so teach them well!

I realise now that when I used to present, everything I did was tailored to my own personality style. I didn't know that other people with a different personality style mix needed to digest the information in different ways. I didn't know that in order to engage, persuade and inspire them I needed to use my preferred style AND tap into other style types too. Happily, one day I attended an Insights Discovery® Personal Style training and began to see the error of my ways. (As well as spotting a career path of training that really appealed to me!)

From that moment on I began to work on my own personal development, increase my flexibility and work towards my new goal to be a trainer. When I was 37, I left corporate life to start my own presentation skills training business and later became an Insights Discovery® Licensed Practitioner and Motivational Maps Practitioner to add depth to my understanding of people's communications and motivation preferences.

## Most people already give 'presentations' or should!

From my experience of working with Executives, Senior Managers, Business Owners and their teams, so many people tell me they 'don't give presentations'. Some are actively avoiding presentations; they are missing opportunities to become more visible within the organisation. But that aside, let's say they are in the type of role where they don't give traditional presentations, standing in front of an audience using PowerPoint. I'd argue that they are still giving presentations. By our definition, a presentation can be:

- ✓ A team talk in the office before the day begins.
- ✓ A new product launch to the sales team.
- ✓ A pitch to a prospective buyer.
- ✓ Attending an industry conference and introducing yourself to new people (networking).
- ✓ A video on your website.
- ✓ A training programme to teach new skills.
- ✓ A teleconference with international colleagues.
- ✓ A team coaching session.
- ✓ A one-to-one meeting with your boss.
- ✓ A webinar with associates.

- ✓ A PR launch.

- ✓ A TV or radio interview.

- ✓ A telephone call with customers.

- ✓ A birthday or leaving speech.

- ✓ An award acceptance.

… and I could go on. The list is endless. When I use the term 'presentation', I mean any form of speaking in public (other than to yourself)! Everyone in business 'presents'.

## Push vs. Pull – which are you?

I've been training professionals to communicate effectively with their specific audience for years; to know their style and preferences and then to be able to identify the Presenter Personality Styles of the audience and adapt their approach accordingly. This is the foundation of good communications, good marketing and sales, great fundraising, teaching, persuading and inspiring. Yet people who do these things perfectly well in other areas of their life and career seem to use them less when in presentations, meetings or talks, and go into 'tell' mode. They try to push their information at people. This is a very old-fashioned approach, yet it is rife in organisations – large and small alike – in the UK and across the Western world.

Instead, High Performance Presentations (and most communications) work better when they 'pull' the audience in, so they want to listen and are asking you for more.

*I'm telling you about what I want you to know*

*I'm sharing with you what I think you want to know*

Soon Millennials will be 50% of the workforce in the UK, and Generation Z will follow on – they especially don't respond well to being told they need to be engaged. Millennials, Generation Z or not, we tend to prefer a 'pull' approach. None of us like to be told what to do!

The pull approach ultimately encourages empowerment, so if you notice a lack of empowerment around you, this could be part of the reason – you aren't taking people on the journey with you. This becomes more and more relevant as the balance of power in business moves more and more to individuals and workers – through social media and websites such as Glass Door, TripAdvisor and Twitter – rather than organisational leaders.

Do you plan your presentations around what the audience wants to hear? Or do you (like most people before I've worked with them) present what you want to tell them?

## Telltale signs you may not be giving engaging, persuasive and inspiring presentations yet

In my unique position as a presentation skills trainer and mentor I've worked with many business leaders and HR professionals who want their people to become better presenters and communicators. I've pulled together some of the common themes into a tick list (which is by no means exhaustive) of hints, winks and secret code which when translated might mean you or your team are not yet delivering High Performance Presentations. Tick all that apply to you or your teams:

Have you in the last year or two ...

### Suffered from nerves which impact your presence e.g.

- ☐ Taken beta blockers or other medication to help you to cope with public speaking?
- ☐ Avoided a promotion or new role because you knew it would involve presenting?
- ☐ Tried delegating a presentation for the wrong reasons?
- ☐ Felt nervous or sick at even the thought of presenting?
- ☐ Bored the audience to near sleep status?
- ☐ Displayed off-putting body language like pacing up and down when speaking, waving your hands around with no purpose or displayed a nervous twitch?
- ☐ Avoided looking into the audience, thus reducing engagement and damaging trust levels?

HIGH PERFORMANCE PRESENTATIONS

- ☐ Adopted annoying habits, like jingling change in the pocket, playing with accessories, or clicking pens?
- ☐ Found yourself putting on an 'act' when it is time to present?
- ☐ Read from slides or a script which makes you face the screen/script thus:
    - o Reducing eye contact, preventing voice projection and variation?
    - o Conveying a lack of subject matter knowledge?
    - o Contributing to incorrect words, punctuation or pronunciation errors?
- ☐ Stopped and run off stage or asked, *'Can I start again?'*
- ☐ Been told you would *'benefit from an increase in executive presence'*?
- ☐ Suffered from a disturbed night's sleep days before an important presentation?

## Not been crystal clear when presenting? e.g.

- ☐ Rushed through it and spoken way too quickly?

- ☐ Lost your place in a presentation and told everyone you'd forgotten or had to ad lib to cover it up?

- ☐ Missed out key points you had planned to cover?

- ☐ Completed insufficient audience research – perhaps you didn't know who the audience were, their current level of knowledge or what they wanted?

- ☐ Taken too long to get to the point, waffled or not got to the point at all?

- ☐ Made mistakes in your presentations which spiralled into something worse?

- ☐ Not being clear on the direction/purpose of the talk for example, when giving someone else's presentation?

- ☐ 'Winged' a presentation without giving it much thought?

- ☐ Run over time in a presentation by more than 5 minutes without being aware of it, or having the audience's permission to do so?

## Not tailored your message to engage and inspire? e.g.

- ☐ Not appreciated why the audience are asking specific questions; not seeing a (predictable) question or generally not answered questions as well as you'd like?

- ☐ Felt frustrated that discussions or questions become a runaway train?

- ☐ With the benefit of hindsight, realised that you hadn't anticipated obvious issues, considered the impact across departments or got down to the numbers/money side of things?

- ☐ Found your projects or launches taking longer than they should; suffered from 'unforeseen issues' or lack buy-in and ownership?

- ☐ Had stakeholders question or doubt your credibility?

- ☐ Experienced the audience not taking the action you requested – could you have been clearer or addressed their objections to action more effectively?

- ☐ Misread the audience – perhaps pitching at too low (or too high) a strategic level, not realising when people weren't following you or assuming silence from the quieter folk is the same as agreement and buy in?

- ☐ Received feedback that you need to increase (or decrease) your assertiveness levels?

I'm not aiming for perfection - this book isn't about becoming a professional speaker, it's about getting the best results for you, your team and your organisation. It's about turning off your autopilot, slowing down, preparing for what you want to communicate and then choosing to respond accordingly in a manner that is best for the audience.

The kind of thing that is easily forgiven (as long as you aren't a professional speaker) when done infrequently is:

- ✓ Computer powering off briefly.
- ✓ Forgetting to click a slide.
- ✓ Needing a few seconds to gather your thoughts.
- ✓ Quietly visiting your notes.
- ✓ Muddling up a few words.
- ✓ A few ums and errs if the message is still clear.

If you ticked some things on the earlier list, then the techniques that follow will help you. If this looks like it could be relevant to members of your team, read on for their sakes (and yours – the success of your team is also your success).

## How to use this book

### Focus on your quick wins first

If you were working with us on a one-to-one basis, we'd look at your current presentation style, skills and approach and easily pinpoint how you could improve – both the quick wins and the long term incremental changes. Because this is a book, not a one-to-one programme, I can't do that so easily, so I've developed a different, non-scientific way to help instead.

In order for you to tailor a solution to your needs and uncover quick wins and incremental improvements, use the tick list from the last section to see where you can improve and combine that with my Presenter Personality Styles (PPS) in Chapter 2 so you can see which unique blend seems most like you. Then, if you choose to, you can use all that information to apply the advice in this book effectively to your individual development.

In the absence of that information you might:

1. Be overwhelmed instead of easily prioritising.

2. Be biased towards your preferred approach and miss your blind spots.

3. Not appreciate what other Presenter Personality Styles (in your audience) might want from a presentation.

## HPPs need the right skillsets, toolsets and mindsets

In order to deliver engaging, persuasive and inspiring presentations you'll firstly want to have a beneficial mindset or helpful 'attitude' - something many people lack when it comes to presentations. Second you'll need the best toolsets like the best way to structure and plan your presentations. And finally you'll need amazing skillsets like personal impact. As we go through the book we'll cover each of these in turn. I have split them for the sake of this book, but of course the lines between the three elements are more blurry in real life! You may notice I've changed skill sets to skillsets for consistency with toolsets, mindsets, even though technically it is two words.

As you go through, keep an open mind. Try the ideas on for

size. Once you've done that, you can take what fits you and leave what doesn't. It really is about you and your individual style – but polished up to the very best you can be so you can always (regardless of deadlines) deliver engaging, persuasive and inspiring presentations.

I have a feeling some of you might be tempted to skip over the section on mindsets and go straight to the action – the skillset section – but that's where the first mistake is made! My approach is unique in many ways, but largely because I deal with mindsets first. Mindsets – our thinking and our beliefs – are powerful things. Just knowing what to do is not enough. Why else would the diet industry be such a money-making machine? If it was all about skillsets then once we all knew the 'right' things to eat and how to exercise, we'd all be the ideal weight, right? But it's not all about skillsets. Often our unhelpful mindsets get in the way.

Once you have read about how to create the most helpful mindset, use the results from the Presenter Personality Style quiz to help you identify what blend of the four Presenter Personality Styles you are. Then as you go through the book there is information on the strengths and weakness of each, so you'll know where to focus your time, efforts and development.

## Connect with the Success Stories

Scattered through the book are four success stories of people with different Presenter Personality Styles, to help you see these techniques come to life. Whilst the names and situations have been adapted to protect client confidentiality, they are all based on a blend of true stories. See what parts of the stories resonate with you and identify what you can learn from that.

## *What next?*

### Instant improvement

Will you see an instant improvement? Yes, on some things you will. Other things might take a little longer to digest and become automatic, but the sooner you start, the sooner you'll achieve your goals. I often tell my clients: 'It's not about perfection but self-correction.' – continual improvement is the aim of the game, and to do that you need to know where you are now and where you'd like to be instead. So, let's take a look at where you are now.

### Rule breakers

This book contains tools, skills and general advice that will work for most of the people most of the time – but there are always exceptions, and everyone is an individual. We all know someone who breaks all the public speaking 'rules' with outrageous success! Keep an open mind and 'test drive' these ideas then select those that work best for you.

### In a hurry?

You can use this book in several ways. Of course, I prefer that you read it cover to cover so as not to miss a thing! But if you want to hone in on the areas most relevant to you, using the Presenter Personality Style, beginning in Chapter 2, will guide you to your strengths, weaknesses and appropriate techniques.

If you don't follow the mindsets and recommendations from this book, you may not fulfil your personal, business or team potential. You'll be fuelling that low bar of public speaking and creating a culture where poor presentations prevail.

But when you take onboard these tips and approaches, even before you've finished this book you can begin to implement the techniques in your daily work life. I'd also love for you to share your learnings with your friends, family and teams to help them deliver HPPs in their organisations.

Let's move on and begin with a personality style quiz, to discover your personal presentation preferences mindset. These will inform the specific presentation skillsets that will be useful for you to focus on and develop, as you move through the book.

HIGH PERFORMANCE PRESENTATIONS

# Chapter 2
# Presenter Personality Style

## *Why get to know your Presenter Personality Style?*

Before we begin on the detail of how to give High Performance Presentations, it's good to know about yourself, so, I'm going to share four Presenter Personality Styles with you. We all have all four styles within our mindsets to a greater or lesser extent. Some styles we tend to prefer over others and they resonate more with us. If you can identify your preferences, it will give you guidance on what skillsets you can improve as you go through the book. The preferences will also help you to ask yourself difficult questions: do you do the things I suggest which are common for that Presenter Personality Style? If you are really honest with yourself, is there room for improvement?

In order for you to establish your dominant (autopilot) type, soon I'm going to invite you to take a (non-scientifically generated) quiz. (If you would like to work with a more detailed, scientifically tested personality style model – find out more about our Presentation Strengths and Weaknesses Identifier on our website here:

www.SimplyAmazingTraining.co.uk/presentation-strengths-weaknesses-identifier/

As a result of the quiz you'll see where you already are and what your potential weaknesses might be in relation to your top one or two styles.

You'll also get to see what your strengths are, so you can play more to them, and perhaps help teach others how to build on those strengths.

There are many profiling tools available and they are very useful to help us generalise and learn about different approaches. But we are only generalising, so not everything about the type will suit you; it is a useful starting point, however, to tailor the approach for you in absence of me being in the same room as you.

## Do I really need to take the quiz?

In theory it isn't necessary to use this Presenter Personality Style quiz. You could just read through the book and decide for yourself which areas you need to work on. The problem with this is you might miss your blind spots – the very things you need to be working on to make the biggest difference to inspire those around you!

When you use the Presenter Personality Style approach sensibly, i.e. looking at your range of types (say your top two) and picking out when advice applies to you or not, taking and leaving the generalisations, you'll make the biggest impact in the shortest time because you'll be working on the right things, being efficient in your personal development and using your time effectively.

## *Presenter Personality Style quiz*

Avoid over-thinking this – just quickly answer these five questions to discover your presentation personality style mix.

1. **Your CEO asks you to give a presentation next week, to update them on your recent projects. Do you:**

    A. Welcome the opportunity with open arms, and consider asking for extra time because you have so much to say?

    B. Want to spend time getting a grip on how you can ensure all your team get the recognition they deserve?

    C. Start to think about how you can gather all the facts and relevant information in time?

    D. Say *'no problem'* and wing it on the day (you're busy after all)?

    E. Immediately develop a cough, in order to pull a convincing sickie and avoid the presentation next week?

2. **You are asked to interview for your ideal job, which involves delivering a 20-minute presentation to a panel about why you are the best candidate? Are you:**

    A. Excited at the prospect of talking to so many people and showing them what you can do?

    B. Feeling a little apprehensive about speaking about yourself for all that time? You'd feel more comfortable if it was a more informal meeting?

C. Beginning to realise that PowerPoint will be your only company for the next two weeks as you prepare to give a factual, thorough presentation showing all your results data?

D. Looking forward to telling them why you are great for the role, and better than the competition (whilst hoping they don't take too long so you can get to your next meeting)?

E. Thinking it will be a nightmare and a waste of time, as you won't get the job anyway?

3. **Your industry body asks you to speak at their annual conference, where there will be competitors and customers. Do you:**

A. Say yes immediately, knowing you will be able to network, impress your peers and improve your career prospects (even before you know the talk topic)?

B. Consider who else in the team might like to present alongside or instead of you, and who else might benefit from the opportunity?

C. Say you'll get back to them, as you need to check your schedule to ensure you have time for research and appropriate preparation before committing?

D. Say you'd love to, then forget all about it until a few days before – you're pretty good at getting your key messages across concisely.

E. Put off saying yes while you think of polite ways to say no or find someone (anyone!) else to give the presentation?

4. **The previous speaker is poorly so, with just three days notice, your good friend asks you to give a speech to 150 guests at their upcoming wedding reception. Your first reaction is:**

   A. To feel excited that you'll get to meet so many people and they can listen to you and your jokes?

   B. To well up – what an honour to be asked. Then to begin to feel the pressure, as it's such a big responsibility and you don't want to let your friend down?

   C. To delay any immediate decision - three days isn't long enough to prepare and gather all the dates and facts on your best friend's past is it?

   D. To say yes, no problem, and then decide how to get the best result in the shortest time?

   E. Panic, panic, panic! Start to feel sick and dizzy already?

5. **You have just delivered a presentation to colleagues and a board member asks you how it went. Do you say:**

   A. Really well, thanks. I got a few laughs and none of the audience were asleep?

   B. Well, thanks for asking, do you have time for a coffee so we can discuss this, and I can share the feedback from the team?

C. It was good but I'm not sure I gave them enough information or that they understood all the details and specifics?

D. Good thanks. I told them what I needed to?

E. I was awful - please don't make me give a presentation ever again!?

## *Presenter Personality Style results*

Calculate which style A, B, C, D or E is most like you, second, third and least like you. Even if you answered all 5 out of 5 the same letter, you won't be only that one style. Take a look through the other answers now, and rank which would have been your second, third, fourth and least likely answers. I said this is non-scientific, so go for it. Ultimately, I'd like to know your order for all five – then read the following in order of your personal blend. As you read through, highlight the areas that you think might be most appropriate for you. You can then repeat this with your team members if they are up for it!

### If the quiz came out as mostly 'A's your style is Sociable

This style tends to be more extraverted and probably enjoys presenting. They like to persuade others with feelings, not just facts, and like presentations to be light-hearted, entertaining and fun. If this is high in your mix, throughout the book look for the word '**Sociable**', indicating where you might want to pay particular attention, in order for others to take on board your ideas more often, and get even better results.

Take a look at your next preferred style now.

### If the quiz came out as mostly 'B's your style is Caring

This style tends to be more introverted naturally (though they may have learned extraverted traits) and they persuade others with feelings, not just facts. They probably prefer a smaller, more informal approach to communicating, rather than formal, stand-up presentations. They like to consider the people and team elements in all they do and tend to influence those around them to consider the fairest approach.

If this is high in your mix, throughout the book look for the word '**Caring**', indicating where you could focus your attention to get a better outcome for yourself and those around you.

Take a look at your next preferred style now.

### If the quiz came out as mostly 'C's your style is Information

This style tends to prefer introversion and likes to take time to consider the relevant research, information and facts. They persuade with facts over feeling. They may prefer not to present, but if they do they will want to have done plenty of preparation and include all the data and facts to help people come to the right decision. If this is high in your mix, throughout the book look for the word '**Information**', which guides you through processes and techniques to improve your skills and advance your presentations accordingly.

Take a look at your next preferred style now.

### If the quiz came out as mostly 'D's your style is Results

This style tends to be more naturally extraverted and prefers to use facts and data above emotional arguments when they influence and present. They like to present top line and to keep it brief and then leave, allowing them to move onto the next thing. If this is high in your mix, throughout the book, look for the word '**Results**', indicating shortcuts to information that will help you get better results, more quickly, from your future presentations.

Take a look at your next preferred style now.

## If the quiz came out as mostly 'E's your style is Monkey

Monkey isn't really a Presenter Personality Style. It is included in the quiz to identify people who are nervous of presenting. If you came out as Monkey, you're really not a comfortable presenter, so if presenting is required a lot in your job, you might be nervous or stressed a great deal of the time. You may be taking far too much time preparing or learning presentations by heart and you probably hate last minute changes. You probably spend too long and waste too much energy on this part of their role. You may even be overworking as a result.

Actually, you may be surprised to learn that underneath your fear and worry you will naturally be one of the four personality styles mentioned above. The thing is you might not be able to see or access that yet, as the fear and worry is overriding and won't let you.

You may have made an art of presentation avoidance, and therefore do too little, too last minute or no preparation/practice. But consider whether you want to remain like that forever. What message are you sending to others? And can you really keep coming up with excuses without people noticing a pattern?

If this is you, and you are reading this, then you know it is time to get over your fear now! Then, once you are confident, you may even enjoy it! I suggest you get started using my other book 'Taming Your Public Speaking Monkeys' to overcome that fear or book onto a programme with us,

www.SimplyAmazingTraining.co.uk/presentation-skills-training/

and then re-take this quiz, to find out which mix of the other four styles is the real you now the Public Speaking Monkeys are 'Tamed'. Then you can continue to work towards delivering High Performance Presentations. There is more about Public Speaking Monkeys in the next Chapter too.

## *Your Presenter Personality Style Mix in more detail*

Once you've read about your preferred style – the one you scored your #1 – double check to see if after reading the styles in fact one of the others is actually your top. (It is non-scientific remember). Next decide your mix preference, then read the other styles that are a bit like you as there may be elements to learn from those too.

For example, I might be **Sociable** first, **Results** second, **Caring** third and **Information** last. This means that as I read the **Sociable** description below I will have many of those traits, as I read **Results** I'll probably recognise some of the traits and behaviours and perhaps a sprinkling of **Caring** traits. It is unlikely I'll share any of the **Information** styles traits naturally (unless I've consciously worked to improve them). But to give engaging, persuasive and inspiring presentations I'll want to learn how to demonstrate traits from those styles that are least like me too – this book will help.

## Sociable – strengths and areas to develop

You embrace the opportunity to speak in front of others, and are likely to be a confident, energetic and entertaining presenter. Because you are **Sociable** and expressive, your passion is contagious. Some people might find your creative approach too informal, however, so be aware of your surroundings.

Whilst you are usually very optimistic, if you're having a bad day – oh dear! – you have a tendency to show it. You may benefit from learning how to manage your emotions, so you can put things aside for the sake of your audience.

Your presenting style is informal, enthusiastic, animated and often humorous. Be careful – this may overwhelm more introverted types. You might benefit from slowing down and toning down both your voice and body language.

If you're not particularly task-orientated, make yourself focus more on how the audience can use what you are communicating in real life – help them apply the learnings.

You are likely to be able to motivate others towards a vision for the future or new idea. You are a fast-paced thinker, but be careful that your style doesn't come across to some as disorganised and difficult to follow. Make sure your imagination doesn't run away with you – use the structure (shown later) to help you improve your clarity of message.

The sort of behaviours that may be getting in the way of you delivering High Performance Presentations are highlighted throughout this book, including the potential to:

- ✗ Be unstructured, difficult to follow and lack clarity.
- ✗ Share impractical ideas without the supporting detail.
- ✗ Unconsciously look low status due to your preference for informality and playing the joker.

You may find it beneficial to live and breathe the concept that 'the presentation isn't about you, it's about the audience'. Take particular note of the audience preparation section and structure chapters.

## Caring – strengths and areas to develop

This means that you are likely to be relaxed, informal, patient and agreeable. But if you say yes when you mean no, you might just be too agreeable. Make sure you are clear and direct in your presentations, especially about the action you'd like the audience to take.

You are very democratic and think everyone should get a say, so make sure that if you are presenting a proposal you are clear about your recommendations. If you come across as too 'wishy washy' you run the risk of someone else taking charge of your presentation.

You are a great listener and great shoulder to cry on, so beware that your natural style of wanting to hear everyone's views doesn't turn into an overrunning Questions and Thoughts section or an impromptu therapy session!

You place a large focus on other people, their feelings and relationships. It's unlikely you'll miss a trick there and you'll be the one spotting other people's faux pas. You'll want to ensure you are sharing with the data-driven types all the information and facts they need to make a decision.

You would feel just as happy if others were to present instead of you. When you do present, you feel a strong sense of duty – you want to represent the organisation or team well. Try not to worry too much about what others think, or you may come across as overly sensitive. When you are confident, you are good at getting the audience onside by sharing the emotional benefits of your story and getting everyone to feel engaged.

Sometimes you might have to deliver difficult news, in which case, use your strength in openness and empathy to get to the point quickly without smoke and mirrors, and show the audience you care and appreciate what they are going through.

The sort of things that may be getting in the way of you giving a High Performance Presentation every time are highlighted throughout this book, including the potential to:

- ✗ Speak too quietly, especially with larger audiences or when you are less confident in your subject matter.
- ✗ Unconsciously look low status due to your preference for everyone to be equal.
- ✗ Invite too much debate and looking to others as if you lack strong opinions.

You may find it beneficial to work on your executive presence: rightly or wrongly, books are judged by their covers!

## Information – strengths and areas to develop

You may prefer written communication to giving a presentation. You are a deep thinker, and like to be analytical, detail-focussed and precise. You work more effectively with facts and figures than emotions. Beware that your need to think deeply doesn't come across as aloofness when on stage. You may want to bring more energy to your talks, as sticking to the facts can get a little tedious for some.

You will be limited by time in a presentation, so you won't be able to give all the detail. You may need to work on narrowing down the key points, and telling a story with the information, not just passing on data.

You are very organised and possess good time-management skills. However, when it comes to presentations, you might have a tendency to over-prepare. The *correct* preparation needn't take as long as you spend, and dare I say it, could achieve better results.

You might not be great at thinking on your feet. If you are asked a question, you like to have all the facts, and then logically put together a suitable answer. Not everyone requires as much detail in an answer as you do! Depending on who you are presenting to, bear in mind some styles can become impatient with lengthy consideration times and such a deliberate approach.

Your arguments are rational, but you may need to work on adding stories into your presentations. It's not 'waffle'; it appeals to all audience styles and can simplify the message.

The obstacles that could be blocking you from giving High Performance Presentations are highlighted throughout this book including the potential to:

- ✘ Start with the detail and not paint the wider, bigger picture of the presentation (some people may see this as a lack of 'strategic thinking').

- ✘ Take too long to get to the key points of the presentation; coming across as too cautious, highlighting all the risks in minute detail rather than summarising key issues.

- ✘ Lack variation of expression or appear boring/lacking in passion for the subject. Consider developing your voice tonality by bringing more emotion into your talks.

You may find it beneficial to show data visually and simply, using a mix of line, pie and bar charts. Clearly and succinctly pull out what value your data is to the audience.

## Results – strengths and areas to develop

You are likely to be confident, fast-paced, and keen to get things done. You may speak quickly and move rapidly through your material. While it's good to maintain some pace, beware you're not leaving a whole section of your audience behind. Repeat key messages and pause at important points – you may well benefit from slowing down.

You probably don't prepare much, or at least not as well as you could. The correct preparation needn't take hours, and will probably achieve better results.

Due to your speed, your presentations may lack structure – and structure is important for the audience to process your ideas easily. Proper planning and structure will help you see what level of detail is required, and by whom.

You are likely to have a lot of energy and drive when presenting, but beware that you avoid coming across as intimidating or overpowering to those of a quieter and more thoughtful disposition.

You are good at thinking on your feet. You answer questions easily – though some may say you haven't given the question enough consideration. It's a good idea to leave plenty of pauses and repeat back any questions to demonstrate that you've listened prior to jumping right in with an answer. You may get impatient with people asking 'irrelevant questions', but they wouldn't be asking them if they weren't *important to them*.

The sort of pitfalls you might be more prone to that prevent High Performance Presentations every time are highlighted throughout this book, including the potential to:

- ✗ Not pace the audience – there's more on pacing later, but for now moving too quickly, literally or figuratively, through the material.

- ✗ Have more of a 'tell' style rather than spending time gaining genuine buy-in.

- ✗ Assume silence is buy-in and wonder why no one does what you thought they were going to do.

As a risk-taker, you should be happy to try new things with your presentation. I suggest working on your planning, structure and delivery – so that everyone in the audience can come along on the journey with you. This would translate into even better results, such as sales or sign-ups.

## *Time to take action*

It's a good idea to make a note of areas where you want to improve and tick those off as you progress through the book. Plus, as we cover each topic, the words **'Sociable'**, **'Caring'**, **'Information'** or **'Results'** are highlighted in the text to guide you towards your likely areas to focus on. Keep your eyes peeled!

We all have blind spots, things about our personalities and communication styles that we can't see ourselves. The next step is to check for blind spots. Look at any weaknesses, especially in your first and second personality styles, that you haven't highlighted and double check they don't apply to you. Ask someone you trust to give you honest feedback – do they think any of those weaknesses could be how others (the audience) might perceive you?

## *What next?*

Those who miss this opportunity to use this quiz to help may take a little longer identifying and prioritising the areas to work on and could miss their blind spots.

When you use these quiz results in addition to what you already know and feel, then you'll cover more angles, become more flexible and develop even more effectively.

Now you know your mindset in relation to your style, let's take a look at the mindsets that commonly hold people back from giving High Performance Presentations.

# Chapter 3
# The Relevance of Mindsets

A large proportion of this book focuses on skillsets, and there are some great techniques and approaches that will help you later in this book; but first, let's look at mindsets for speaking success in respect to your verbal communications or those of your teams.

## *Why do I need to know about mindsets?*

A mindset is defined as a particular way of thinking: a person's attitude or set of opinions or beliefs about something.

To make real, long-term improvement, you and your audience need to start with mindset. From our experience, most education and training are focussed on teaching skills. The problem with that is that it assumes any failure in the current situation is only as a result of a lack of knowledge. Drawing a parallel with obesity, that would mean that, as long as everyone is educated on healthy eating and exercise, the problem will disappear – how is that approach going so far? Actually, what is needed is a change in mindset – for people to want to eat healthily and be more active. Only then having skills and knowledge comes into play.

To make a difference in the world, however big or small, you need to help your audience change their mindset from where they are now to where you want them to be. It may involve teaching some skills – but it is rarely solely about skills.

This means that if you want to influence others, persuade

people, gain buy-in to a new approach, win funding for a major project, sell more profitable products or even raise money for a charity, you'll want to be aware of mindset: what mindset the audience currently have, and what mindset you want to help them adopt in order to see your vision. Subsequently if you need to teach some skills, you should find they learn the skills quickly and easily – and actually implement what they've learnt! Mindset affects everything we do.

During my corporate career we often had days out the office doing training and team development – and yes, we bonded more as a team, learnt some new and interesting things, but we rarely effectively applied them when we returned to work. Perhaps for the first week or two, but then the good intentions slipped away. I'm sure you've experienced this. Haven't you?

There were just a few of the trainings and talks that were different – I'd say just 3-5 in over 20 years! Reflecting back, those experiences were truly mindset changing, although I didn't know it at the time. I'd gone in with one attitude (that I may not even have been aware of) and come out with the germination of another more helpful mindset. Over the long term, those changes moved me to help others more effectively, be clearer on my desires and goals and removed obstacles in the way. It took time for these to blossom fully, but the shift was there.

It's these shifts I want you to learn to create in your audience, your team and yourself with your engaging, persuasive and inspiring presentations.

## *Your current mindset*

In this section we'll uncover where you are now with your own attitude or mindset towards presenting, and if you choose to, you can apply everything you've learnt to look at your team members' attitudes too. You'll begin to recognise any less helpful mindsets and then learn new, more enhancing mindsets to replace them.

To improve anything in your life it is important to understand:

1) What your mindset is now.

2) Whether it is helping you to reach your objectives.

3) If not, then what you need your new mindset to be to more easily achieve your objectives.

Spend a few moments considering your honest answer to this question:

> **How do you feel currently about giving a presentation?**

My experience is that answers to this question vary widely, with a few at the extremes of loving it or absolutely hating it and most in the middle somewhere – a good old Bell curve!

## If you absolutely hate it or have a fear of presenting ...

You probably already know it's not helping you. It's probable you have a Public Speaking Monkey (more about these later) and the first thing to do is overcome it. I'll give an overview of how to do this in the forthcoming pages, and if you want more information after that, you can find this in my book, 'Taming

Your Public Speaking Monkeys'. Most of my best-performing clients started off with this monkey mindset and subsequently 'Tamed Their Monkeys' and went on to achieve amazing things, not only presenting confidently, but (for example) winning new contracts at conferences of over 400 people. This sort of success is possible for you too.

## If you're in the middle, between love it and hate it ...

You might have answered something like this:

>'I don't like them but ...'

>'I'd prefer not to do them'

>'I get through it'

>'I've got used to it now'

>'I'm OK'

>'I'm not nervous'

>'I've got better over the years'

Imagine for a moment I had asked that question about a different area of your work. If you were an experienced accountant and I'd asked you how you feel about reading a profit and loss, I can't imagine it would be a great career move if you'd given any of the answers above. The danger zone – the invisible poisonous gas – is this middle mindset, the one where you think you are scraping through but in fact you may be letting yourself down. Lurking underneath these seemingly harmless statements are very likely to be some 'Mini Monkeys' which need taming before you can deliver your best.

You've probably heard the saying that you are only as strong as your weakest link.

> **You are only as strong as your weakest link – are presentations your weakest link?**

## Watch out – if you love presenting ...

I sound like the doom bringer now, but for those who love presenting, beware! You are also in danger! It's great that you have a positive attitude and are free from any nerves or fears but be careful, confidence doesn't always mean competence; there is always room for improvement. Being 'good enough' can often leave people complacent so they forget they need to learn and improve, especially as they climb the career ladder and feedback becomes less frequent.

Most of our clients who have achieved the best results were those who didn't love presenting – they knew they needed to improve so they came with an open mind and they were motivated to learn more and develop. That doesn't mean strong presenters can't experience equally transformative results but to do that, I strongly suggest you approach the information in this book with an open mindset and enjoy applying it to improving all your verbal communications (and in fact many of the techniques can apply to written communications too – not least using the SAS structure later).

## *How to approach mindsets*

## *What next?*

### If you're pushed for time

While all of the mindsets in this book are useful, if you are pushed for time you might choose to only use the quiz to prioritise your learning. That's fine but you may find yourself having to revisit more on mindsets later because if you miss out on understanding your own mindset or that of your teams or your audience, it is less likely you'll achieve the impact you desire.

If you can create the time the best approach is to go through each mindset step-by-step, so read on! When you understand and adapt your mindset 'software' appropriately, the world will be your oyster.

Now you're more aware of your current presentation mindset, let's look at some other ideas around mindset. Let's first look at the most common unhelpful mindsets that prevent people from giving HPPs. Then some more helpful mindsets it would be good to install (a bit like updating your brain's software to improve your capabilities) that are essential to creating and delivering High Performance Presentations.

# Chapter 4
# Low Performance Mindsets

From my experience with clients and researching this book, there are three common mindsets that hold professionals back, not only in their presentations but in their careers and communications generally:

1. Fixed mindset approach.
2. Public Speaking Monkeys.
3. The Downward Spiral.

## *Fixed/inflexible mindset*

With a fixed mindset, people believe their basic qualities, like intelligence or confidence, are simply fixed traits. For speaking, some people are naturally happier to speak in front of others. Some may never have been a fan of speaking. A fixed mindset believes they aren't good at speaking now and *'will never like it or be good'*. The problem with this is that people who believe it miss out on maximising their potential.

**Fixed Mindset exercise**

1) Note down if there are any areas around presenting or communicating where you think you can't change.

2) Note down if there are any areas elsewhere in life where you think you can't change.

3) Imagine you are in a court of law telling a judge that you couldn't change. Would they agree or disagree with you that it was impossible to change?

4) If it is possible to change then in Chapter 5 you'll hear about some more helpful mindsets to adopt instead, specifically adopting a growth mindset.

## Public Speaking Monkeys

Monkeys is the term and metaphor that I've personally created to represent those mind mutterings or voices in your head that tell you *'You're Stupid', 'You're Boring'* or *'You're Not Good Enough'*. Most people have them (whether they admit it or not) from CEOs to construction sales teams and finance directors to doctors. When you put yourself up there in front of others it is a much easier ride if you have 'Tamed All Your Monkeys' so they aren't chattering away, distracting you. It is also the number one thing that will improve your ability to deliver engaging, persuasive and inspiring presentations and hence have a very positive knock on effect onto your career progression too. How do I know that? Because I've helped thousands of people to 'Tame' their Public Speaking Monkeys, and I've seen their careers speed up as a result!

### Why do negative monkeys matter?

I did okay at school but found a few things difficult to learn, like telling the time on an analogue clock. As I think about it now, it was a baffling process. 12.15 and quarter past 12 are the same, when surely a quarter is much smaller than 15? Why is it quarter to 1 and not three quarters to 1? It was illogical. So, when I was asked at junior school to stand up and tell the time, I had no choice but to guess and the class laughed at my answers. My confidence in learning to tell the time diminished dramatically. I gave it less effort and attention and hence I didn't develop that skill as early as I could have.

I also found it impossible to learn my times tables, despite my dad (a dentist!) trying to encourage me with sweets. I realise now that I never learnt a strategy to memorise things and I didn't see the point of learning my times tables – I was, and still am, more of a 'work it out' type. When I was asked to stand up and recite times tables at school, I worked each one out, meaning I was too slow and my motivation diminished. By the way, I *still* don't know my times tables, despite having an A-Level in Maths! But I know that if I wanted to learn them (mindset) then I could find out how (skillset).

Despite these blips, I think I'm a relatively intelligent person, I have a 2:1 degree and was awarded 'Best Marketing Student' upon graduation so I did OK. But I can see how these incidents in my past had given me a Telling-The-Time Monkey and a Maths Monkey. If I'd have gone about learning in a way that suited my learning style, I'm sure I'd have got even better results. I'm over those monkeys now and plenty more, but it's taken me a long time to discover how to love learning, growing and continual improvement.

I've had the privilege of working with many mentoring clients who have opened up and shared their stories of school humiliation with me. They often had a far worse time of it than I did, leaving school with a deeply held belief they were stupid or weren't good enough.

If you are lucky enough to have never experienced this, you may not appreciate that it can – and does – impact people for their whole lives until they address it. Those clients with

'Chunky Monkeys' are incredibly brave to reach a point where they want to resolve these issues with our help.

## Monkeys follow a colour code system

Public Speaking Monkeys follow a traffic light system: red, amber or green.

### Red Monkeys

The most dangerous and damaging can be 'Red Monkeys'. These are where people have a negative belief that is totally not true circling in their head when they even begin to think about presenting. These can be things like, *'You're Not Good Enough'*, *'You'll Look Silly'* or *'You're Stupid'*.

Let's take the *'You're Stupid'* Monkey as an example – this is a Red Monkey. It isn't true – the person is never stupid. I've written a whole other book explaining why and what to do about it, but to keep it brief here:

1. The person will not be able to easily define what a stupid person looks like.

2. When they do list their definition, they will realise that they don't fit that description and therefore consciously know that they aren't stupid.

This is rarely enough to 'Tame The Monkey' – that's a longer process – but at least now we know it is not true.

A Red Monkey is completely untrue, and consciously you know that or can come to see that ... but your unconscious mind (where the monkeys live) still believes *'You're Stupid'* no matter how many affirmations you've tried! Affirmations alone are a bit like trying to beat the monkey into submission. But monkeys are strong and though they may subside while they recover, it's very likely they'll return – and probably at the very worst time!!!

The reason it *is* a monkey is because of the conflict between the two parts of you – the conscious mind that knows it is irrational to think *'You're Stupid'*, and the unconscious mind that keeps reminding you you're stupid. If it were true (whatever 'it' means, and whether we think anyone is 'stupid') then it wouldn't be a monkey. You'd know you were stupid (although you may not like it) and you'd not be in conflict with yourself about it.

Note: monkeys will often pop up elsewhere across life – for example the *'You're Stupid'* Monkey might mean that the individual unconsciously does one or all of the following:

1. Miss out on jobs despite others telling them to apply – because they think they aren't clever enough.

2. (Ironically) have far more qualifications than they really

need – because they are so desperate to prove to themselves or others that they aren't stupid.

3. Avoid speaking up in any group situation – even social situations – because they don't want to get the answer wrong as that will show to others that they are stupid.

4. Spend too long on many tasks – because they don't want to make any mistakes otherwise they, or others, will think they are stupid.

5. Be very competitive in the academic arena (or pub quizzes!) and want to win at all costs – that way they can demonstrate they aren't stupid.

6. Overwork – because they want to show themselves, and those around them they aren't stupid.

Often people with this monkey – and other Red Monkeys – are high achievers because their monkey has been driving them so hard. *'That sounds great!'* I hear you cry, *'They've got a good job'*, yes, perhaps, but people with Red Monkeys may find ...

**They feel they have no choice** – because they feel they must constantly strive to prove they aren't stupid. That can get very tiring. The better place to be is in a situation where, if you choose to work hard on a specific project or for a specific length of time, then you can do so. Equally if a less important project comes along, you can prioritise other things (rather than staying 4 hours late to complete it). 'Taming Your Monkeys' gives you back choice.

**Their work life balance is way off** – things tend to succeed only when focus is put into them. Those with monkeys that cause them to overwork are not as able to put the focus on non-work. As a result, other areas of life such as health or relationships may well decline.

**They are over-sensitive** – if you have a Red Monkey or two lurking around, you can be very critical of yourself. The last thing you need is someone else telling you how stupid you are! The problem is that most of the time they weren't saying anything of the sort, but because of the monkey you're over sensitive and often see or hear remarks or actions as negative.

Let me give you an example: your boss comes along and wants to share a new idea they had on the train to work that day, *'Why don't we change the project to include xyz?'* Unfortunately, if you have a *'You're Stupid'* Monkey you are likely to take that badly, thinking, *'I should have thought of that – how stupid of me'* or, *'I must be stupid because she's got to tell me what to do'*.

Note that so many of these things aren't even presentation skills related – they are life and/or work related. Monkeys affect you in many areas of life, but they aren't always noticeable because you have had a lifetime of practice covering them up. The reason it shows up in the context of presenting is because there really is nowhere to hide: when you are asked to give a presentation it's just you and your monkeys!

We've taken the 'Stupid' Monkey as an example. Each monkey will have its own, perhaps similar side effects.

Red Monkeys are often more visible to other people than the individual themselves – so if you are thinking of suggesting a member of your team gets help then tread carefully! The person doesn't need to know exactly what the monkey is (that is all a part of the 'Taming The Monkeys' process). Simply acknowledging and wanting to eliminate the negative side effects is often sufficiently motivating to encourage the individual to do something about it. Working through the process using my other book or working with our team on a one-to-one basis will help 'Tame Those Monkeys'.

**Green Monkeys**

Green Monkeys are beliefs that are 'true', such as:

- ✗ I don't know how to make accountancy interesting.
- ✗ I don't know how to tell an engaging story.
- ✗ I'm overweight.
- ✗ I have a monotone voice and need more variation.
- ✗ I do not always spell things correctly on the flip chart.
- ✗ I don't know how to structure my talk.
- ✗ I don't know how to be concise.

- ✗ I'm not as tall as other people.

- ✗ My French isn't up to the standard required.

- ✗ I do all my presentations off the cuff.

- ✗ I don't allow enough time to prepare or practise.

Green Monkeys are fine if they hold an appropriate amount of emotion. By that I mean no negative emotions or feelings are attached to that belief. If there is negative emotion, then it's an Amber Monkey that needs to be 'Tamed'.

There are only two things you can do with a genuine Green Monkey:

> Learn a new skill, approach or technique that will help you improve on that monkey.

> Decide not to learn that skill and be genuinely neutral in your emotions about that monkey, knowing it doesn't impact your presentations, or if it does you are prepared to live with that.

For example, you can either learn how to make a topic engaging (or pay someone else to do it) or you can decide not to hold those meetings anyway.

If you are overweight, you can decide to eat the right foods and exercise more and/or choose to accept and be comfortable with your weight as it is.

### *Amber Monkeys*

These are a little more tricky to spot because they have elements of Red and Green Monkey to them. They are both untrue and true. For example, the *'You're Boring'* Monkey. This is often a Red Monkey that needs taming – it is untrue that you are boring – combined with a Green Monkey – it is true that your topic can come across as boring or your presentations can be boring.

You'll know if you have an Amber Monkey because it is unlikely to feel awful, but now it has been pointed out you'll notice that there is something illogical about your fears. With Amber Monkeys you need to 'Tame' them down to Green Monkeys. They don't disappear altogether yet, you are just left with the Green Monkey. Then you either do something about that Green Monkey or know not to let it worry you.

## What issues do Red and Amber Monkeys cause?

The size of a monkey can range from 'Chunky Monkeys' – which usually result in being fearful or nervous about presenting – to 'Mini Monkeys' – which tend to impact performance. A High Performance Presentation is one which is free from big or little hang ups or negative mindsets that will work against you when you are speaking. Whatever sized monkey you have, you need to 'Tame' them because ...

## 1) Public Speaking Monkeys prevent you from fully focussing on the audience.

If you have mind chatter going on you can't be focussed on the audience; you'll be focussed on yourself, which results in a somewhat selfish presentation.

A selfish presentation is one with little or no thought to the audience; it's mostly focussed on what you think and what you do or don't want. Inclusive, interactive and engaging presentations consider and adapt to the audience, for example, considering why they would want to give up their valuable time to listen to you! (This is sometimes known as WIIFM, 'What's in it for me?')

What do they want from the presentation? What do they need to know, how much and at what level? What is the best way to structure the information into easily digestible chunks? What are their existing feelings and mindsets around what you are presenting and where do you want their mindset to be once you've finished? How do you want them to do something differently after the presentation and what questions and objections are they likely to have? And the list goes on! (More on this from Chapter 6 onwards.)

The questions and answers section (or questions and thoughts as you'll discover later) is a Public Speaking Monkey's playground! Monkeys make answering questions professionally tough! If any part of our mind is busy caught up thinking about ourselves when we answer questions, we can't be 100% focussed on giving the audience what they want and need. If you are saying to yourself, *'I hope I don't get asked something I don't know'* or, *'I don't want to look stupid'* when someone asks a question, that's a sign that there are monkeys that need taming.

Instead, you want to be thinking, *'What is the best way I can answer this question in order to help that person (and potentially others in the room) understand*?' To help with this, I will share some top techniques for answering questions later in the book.

> **A selfish presentation is one with no thought to the audience, focussed only on what you think and what you want**

**2) Public Speaking Monkeys often impact upon your ability to seek, act and adapt to feedback.**

We touched upon this earlier. Having worked with many professionals (and their Public Speaking Monkeys!) it is very common for those with the *'You're Not Good Enough'* Monkey, for example, to be very bad at taking on board any kind of feedback. After all, they already have a part of them that feels their presentation isn't good enough, so when someone says anything that could be taken as criticism, that's the way they'll see it. They might also feel that some questions at the end of a presentation are an attack on their presentation or views rather than just questions. Watch out for a tendency to be over-sensitive – if you are over-sensitive, it is likely there is a Public Speaking Monkey or two lurking around which need to be 'Tamed'.

When you're working with others one of the most important things is to demonstrate that you can take on feedback, respond well and adapt. Even if you are receiving feedback that isn't all positive, it's what you do with that feedback that matters.

If you find yourself getting angry, defensive or biting your lip in response to feedback, it is likely there is a Public Speaking Monkey or two to be 'Tamed'!

### 3) Public Speaking Monkeys prevent you from coming across in your natural manner.

You will have seen this many times: the person was perfectly normal whilst sitting down and talking, but then, unconsciously 'put on an act' when they got up to present, or just weren't themselves any more. This results in **unconscious feelings of mistrust** – not great if you want to influence, persuade or sell to the audience.

### What results can be achieved by monkey 'taming'?

'Untamed' Chunky Red Monkeys will sabotage the individual's presentations and career, and at worst, will be impacting across their whole lives.

Taming them can be truly life changing – people present without the nerves, they become a better version of themselves and take on feedback easily, so continually learn and improve – a fulfilling Upward Spiral of success (more about that later).

'Untamed' Green Monkeys, depending on their size, can slowly erode your career prospects. Probably you won't get pulled up on it; it may never get mentioned but you now know you are likely to be holding yourself and your results back.

When you 'Tame' your Green Monkeys you'll be improving your communication skills, increasing your ability to influence and thus be more likely to achieve your goals.

'Untamed' Amber Monkeys, depending on the size, can cause you to go on the Downward Spiral (which we will cover next) during presentations. Others may not be able to see your issue, but you know it is preventing you from achieving your goals.

When you 'Tame' your Amber Monkeys you'll feel calmer inside, be better able to consider the audience outside your head and thus experience more presentation, persuasion and communication success.

In Chapter 5 you'll see what approaches you can take to address any of these negative mindsets.

## *The Downward Spiral*

A Downward Spiral can look like this: before the presentation has even begun (and in some cases even months before) the presenter begins to worry and lose sleep. So instead of spending time preparing, they waste time hoping it will go away. They then leave the preparation to the last minute (they were hoping they wouldn't have to do it after all) and are not likely to know how to prepare efficiently (they've not wanted to find out because they hate presenting and haven't done very much of it).

When it comes to the start of the presentation, even before they have said a word, the audience can see the presenter is nervous (they look scared, avoid eye contact and nervously grasp their hands and notes). In response the audience stop smiling and wait nervously too. The presenter dares to look up to see a sea of unsmiling, uncomfortable faces.

As the presenter speaks they go too quickly (they are in a rush to get it over and done with), their throat goes dry (because they are going too quickly and not breathing correctly) and of course they didn't think to have water nearby.

They keep looking down at their notes (or the screen) and thus fail to connect with the audience. If they do happen to look up, they see a disconnected look on the faces of those 'listening' and so assume they are bored. Now they speed up further and rush through the remaining slides as fast as possible.

Therefore, I call it the Downward Spiral – because it just keeps getting worse and each little thing builds on the next to make the presentation pretty poor! The only thing the presenter and the audience have in common is that they are glad it's over!

## HIGH PERFORMANCE PRESENTATIONS

*Negative Monkey Voices*

don't prepare
try to avoid
don't practise
looks nervous
audience feels nervous
dry throat
read notes
glance up
see 'bored' audience
go too fast
**Poor Presentation**

Can you imagine what that must feel like for someone with monkeys? That might be a member of your team now, but they might never tell you. Perhaps you can help as you recognise some of the signs – they look nervous, speak too quickly or cling for dear life to the script. They might read from the PowerPoint slides for fear of making any mistakes.

There is no point asking them to *'be more confident'*, *'slow down'* or *'stop reading from the slides'*. You've probably asked them to do this before, but they won't – not until their monkeys are 'Tamed'!

Even confident people can feed the Downward Spiral - imagine this scenario: you've been asked to do another presentation, but you have too much 'real' work to be getting on with – how are you meant to get all your work done if you have to keep preparing and giving presentations all the time? So, you decide to recycle the PowerPoint deck the Marketing Team used last year and change a few slides. You don't spend any time thinking about the audience and what they need. You don't consider that the presentation you are adapting may not be all that good in the first place. You don't ask how the previous presentation went. You may not consider the changes in market, technology or attitudes since the last presentation. You won't have adapted the content for the time, location or context of the meeting, you won't get your tone across as they are someone else's slides and you certainly won't come up with any unique or creative communication techniques or ideas because you haven't put in the time or energy.

I know some of you are thinking, *'Well it's just the (fill in the gap). I don't have to impress them with my presentation. I'll just get it over and done with.'* Error!!! Let's use an example, say an induction programme for a bunch of newbies. Who do the newbies often get to talk to? The CEO or Head of HR – they may be asked for their formal or informal feedback. Imagine instead if these newbies, when asked, *'Have you enjoyed the day so far'* all said, *'Yes especially the xyz presentation on ... It really inspired me to think about ...'* Now that would get you and your team noticed for all the right reasons!

Learn how to be on the Upward Spiral in the next chapter.

## *How to know if there are negative mindsets lurking*

If you still aren't sure if you have a negative mindset that is working against you, ponder these questions and see where you or your team might want to improve. Do you or your team:

- Enjoy presenting as much as the rest of the role?
- Feel neutral or positive when asked to present?
- Leave presentations to the last minute knowing that you should have allowed more time?
- Over or under prepare?
- Feel nervous (not flowing with adrenaline) before you start or in the first few minutes?
- Have any illogical beliefs, like believing any of the following will make it better or worse: A larger/smaller audience, presenting to strangers/friends, presenting to senior or junior colleagues or presenting to more or less knowledgeable audiences?

If you recognise any negative mindsets, make a note of them and read the next chapter to see the more helpful mindsets to adopt instead.

No negative mindsets? Read the next chapter to understand more about the positive mindsets you've probably already adopted. This will help you to understand yourself better and help you to help your team, and those around you, to adopt these approaches too.

## *What next?*

If you notice any of these most common low performance mindsets (or others I've not mentioned) in yourself or your teams it's an appropriate time to change now. Alternatively, you risk negatively impacting not only your own abilities to communicate but also that of those around you.

If you decide to change your mindsets now, by reading and implementing the concepts in the next chapter, then you'll lay the foundations of success for yourself, your teams and your organisation. Many clients even say that in addition to their presentations improving, so has their outlook to a lot of other things too. The helpful mindsets in this book are related to presentations but if you choose to adopt them in other areas of life too, all the better!

But before that, let's look at the first of four 'Success Stories', and keep an eye out for his negative mindset and new positive one specifically.

## *Success Story – Simon Sociable*

Simon was a larger-than-life character with a postgraduate degree, plus an MBA. He was passionate about his role as Managing Director. He was a great networker, he loved talking to people (and the hind legs off a donkey) and was great at selling and public relations. But when it came to giving more official speeches he'd lose all his personality. He'd get the basic message across but didn't inspire people with his presentations (unlike in 'real life'). The Exec didn't understand how he could be so confident normally, but so bland when he presented (but because they couldn't do any better, they never pushed him). Simon's personality style is **Sociable** preference, followed by **Results**, then **Caring**, with **Information** his least preferred style.

This was a big year for the business – they wanted to raise capital to put into a new product idea, but they needed to convince investors to part with their money. Simon knew he could convince them on a one-to-one basis; he'd done it before. But this new approach meant he had 10 minutes to present to a panel of 7 investors in a lecture theatre style room with an audience of entrepreneurs listening!

Simon came to us for help specifically with this project in mind and, after reading about 'Public Speaking Monkeys', we worked together and uncovered one of the more ironic (but still common) monkeys. Simon's Red Monkey, from all the way back in school, was telling him he was stupid. Simon knew he wasn't stupid (and happily 'untamed monkeys' don't often speak the truth) but we went to work to 'Tame' this monkey. Why is it ironic you might ask? Turns out he was clever and always top of his class – so he was put up a year. But no one explained that *meant that overnight he would no longer be top of the class and might even be towards the bottom for a little while, as he began to catch up. Little was he aware, until we worked together, that such a positive event caused such a negative monkey.*

*After changing his mindset to a more positive and constructive one, Simon was delighted to learn all the new toolsets and skillsets needed to deliver High Performance Presentations. What he liked best was the Simply Amazing Structure™ (SAS).*

- *Being Sociable style preference, Simon previously didn't care much for structure; he'd prefer to do off the cuff informal talks. Using the SAS we showed him, he learnt how to bring structure and clarity to a message, yet retain enough freedom to tell his little anecdotes along the way without running over time.*

- *Simon learnt how to be succinct – something he knew would benefit him everywhere, not just in his formal presentations. He would never have known that his old 'You're Stupid' Monkey contributed to his over-talking because he felt he had to explain everything he knew to everyone – thus showing he wasn't stupid! Now he explains just enough in relation to the audience's needs, not his own.*

- *He also realised that to see more success he needed to adapt his style to the audience. His dominant character was wonderful in most situations, but he learnt what others wanted, and now knew he needed to 'tone it down' a bit to make the more introverted styles less overwhelmed by his intensity. The best way for his message to influence was when he calmed down and slowed down whilst retaining his passion.*

*Simon worked on his Green Monkeys – after some solid preparation and gaining feedback from the team in the development of the SAS, he practised his presentation for the first time EVER! He used his time wisely, focussing on his key messages and practising appropriate accompanying hand movements (instead of his old windmill hands!)*

*Days before the big event, Simon felt ready. On the day, he felt adrenaline because it was a big deal, literally, but he didn't feel those old monkeys. Because of that, the presentation to the investment panel went better than Simon could have imagined – he answered all the questions easily and openly. They loved his collaborative approach; they could sense he was open and not hiding anything from them. Of course, the Chairman was delighted with seeing the real Simon blossom too. Needless to say they got the capital they wanted and more besides.*

# Chapter 5
# High Performance Mindsets

The antidote to the three most common negative mindsets are adopting a growth mindset, adopting 'Helpful Monkeys' and staying on the Upward Spiral.

## *Growth Mindset*

### Why adopt a growth mindset?

In a growth mindset, people believe that their most basic abilities can be developed through dedication and hard work – brains and talent are just the starting point. This view creates a love of learning and a resilience that is essential for great accomplishment. Virtually all great people have had these qualities.

I believe everyone can improve and everyone can become a good – and perhaps great – speaker. Perhaps not everyone can be Barack Obama (though he did put in a lot of practice!) but certainly you can achieve very high standards, should you choose to, with some focussed effort up front and some small/quick continual improvements over time.

### What mindsets underpin a growth mindset?

To support the growth mindset a collection of supporting mindsets is needed and I want to take you through each of those now. I have collected these from the world of NLP (Neuro Linguistic Programming) and I find they help clients no end. And the beauty is (for the sceptics out there) you don't need to even believe these mindsets, you just need to act as if they were true! (I'll give you some time to get your head around that one!)

## Perfection isn't the aim!

### Continual improvement

Darren Hardy wrote a great book on this topic called 'The Compound Effect'. He says, *'small seemingly insignificant changes made consistently over time make a massive impact'*. For example, if you aren't a natural planner but just commit to spending a few minutes preparing for every meeting it will make a massive difference over time. I strive to use this principal in my life, training and with all my coaching clients.

I had the pleasure, several years ago, of working for Toyota Motor Europe for over 6 months on a bespoke training programme. They were masters of continual improvement – or 'Kaizen', as they called it. Even the training course I wrote was pretested so it could be improved upon. It was a 5-day Train the Trainer course and a representative panel sat through the 5-day course before the participants, in order to improve it! How cool is that? Each improvement was relatively small and would not necessarily be noticeable on its own, but when added up across the topics and the days, it led to a significant improvement.

When it comes to developing your presentation style, you can use this approach to improve just one small thing each time. Perhaps you'll think about improving interactivity and implement that daily for a week in all your communications.

By continually improving you are reducing the chances of a big mistake because you are catching things early. However, if you do notice that whatever you are doing isn't working with the audience, then you need to do something different – as soon as possible. And if that doesn't work, try something else. This means you have to be aware enough of your audience to pick up on these minute cues that things aren't going well – way before the yawns start and mobile phones are pulled out!

### *Rename failure and call it feedback*

Everyone makes mistakes and it is OK to do so. Another helpful mindset is that, 'There is no failure only feedback'. Where you might have otherwise seen something as a failure it is far more helpful to see it as feedback – then you can learn from it.

> *'I have not failed. I've just found
> 10,000 ways that won't work.'*
> **Thomas A. Edison**

### *With increased flexibility comes increased success*

If you strive to improve and adapt to the situation, then it makes sense that the more options you have open to you, the greater your flexibility and the wider your choice of approaches, tools and techniques. So, if you come across a challenge or situation that isn't working for you, you will have multiple ways of looking at it, addressing it or overcoming it. That's why the toolsets and skillsets in this book are so useful – you gain more options and increased flexibility.

There is a saying, *'if you always do what you've always done, you'll always get what you've always got'* – but that isn't necessarily true in these fast-changing times. If you always do what you've always done – you might not get anything. You need to have plenty of other options available in case that one doesn't work out. I have seen stand-up comedians and presenters alike roll out exactly the same performance as they did the previous day or week, but get totally different results. To thrive, not just survive, you need to be able to adapt, ideally on the go!

This flexibility needs to be tailored to the audience – who they are and what they want (see audience preparation, Chapter 6 later) – and it's dependant on what you want to achieve. Generally, the more flexible your behaviour and communication, the more likely you are to be able to communicate effectively, and with more people.

Avoid perfection, but be aware enough of what is going on to 'correct' things in the moment (or later) yourself.

> **'Avoid perfection – it's about self-correction.'**
> **Dee Clayton**

To illustrate this point, if you notice your hands are wildly swinging about during presentations for no reason, once you've read this book you'll be more aware of that, and you can self-correct by quietly relaxing them by your side.

If you've said something to break rapport with the audience, assuming you're in Peripheral Vision, then you'll be able to see that in the audience's reactions, and with enough flexibility you can self-correct by changing your approach (more on all this later).

## Take ownership

### *Be responsible for your own results*

Successful people take full responsibility for their own results – good, bad or ugly. Then they can do something about it! They avoid blaming other things, people or the situation. (Remember, these beliefs don't need to be actually true, you just need to act as if they are true; then you become more empowered in your response to the situation.) For example, thinking about a conference speech scenario you could say:

> 'That presentation didn't go well because it was the graveyard shift after lunch.'

The problem with this belief is that it is disempowering – you can do very little about it. You could perhaps ask the organisers not to have the slot after lunch next time, but someone has to. When you take full responsibility for that result, you could have said instead:

> 'As it was after lunch I could have thought about that in advance and spent some time doing an icebreaker – getting them to introduce themselves to someone new, for example. As I saw the audience begin to look tired throughout my presentation I could have included more tag questions to get them involved. Couldn't I?'

(More on tag questions in Chapter 11).

### *The meaning of communication is the response I get*

This belief strategy goes hand in hand with the idea of taking full responsibility for your results and is best explained by an example.

Let's say someone asks you a question and you answer it in a way which you think is polite and effective, but nonetheless that person takes umbrage. Even though you didn't intend that to happen, you appreciate that was the *meaning* of your communication *to them*. The benefit of this new mindset is that then *you* can take 100% responsibility to 'correct' the communication so that it is understood in the way it was intended (rather than it becoming an argument, debate or worse still, silent simmer, none of which resolve the issue).

In another example, let's assume we are inviting people to take action in our presentation. Say we are asking everyone to look at a design and give their feedback through an online questionnaire by Friday. What might happen is that some people will do so, and others may not do it on time or correctly.

We take the view that the meaning of the communication was exactly what we got. So, whilst we might have said that we wanted it completed online by Friday – the *meaning* of the communication, to those who didn't complete it by Friday, was something else. They may have taken a different meaning; they may not have understood the instructions, they may have forgotten or thought the deadline was flexible.

In order to 'correct' this next time, we might want to spend more time checking everyone understands and 'buys into' following the instructions. We might put someone in charge of rounding up the results or set an email reminder in place just before the deadline etc.

Again, the benefit of this belief is that you are 100%

responsible, and are therefore empowered to do something differently, not just sit on your hands and wait.

### *Three fingers back*

I would like you to play a game with me here. If you're in a situation where it's okay to do so, then take your hand now and point at an imaginary audience, whilst saying to them '*You are a tough audience*'. Keep your hand in position.

I'm assuming your index finger is pointing forward – but where are the remaining 3 fingers pointing? The answer is most often, 'Pointing back at me'. I use this to remind us that our communication is often a mirror which reflects back at us.

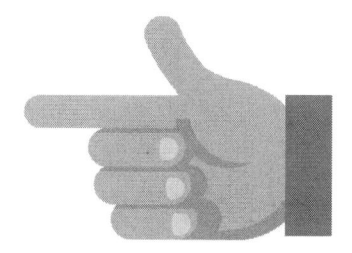

Consider for a moment that a presentation is like a huge mirror reflecting back a magnified version of what we project out. If you want the presentation to go well, project out positives not negatives!

Let's take a look at that in action. If we are thinking how tough, bad and unfriendly the audience are, then those thoughts will reflect in our body language (unless you are a trained actor or spy!) As soon as the audience get a sniff of this they will (unconsciously) react accordingly – you look a bit shifty, so they will mistrust you. Their body language will shift accordingly, and you'll pick up on that, proving yourself right that they are a tough audience! All of that could happen in just a few seconds.

A more helpful mindset is to act as if you believe there is no such thing as a tough, bad or unfriendly audience. There are only audiences with whom you haven't built enough rapport yet. Your job is to build rapport, being as flexible as possible, using as many different techniques as you need, until you are successful. (We'll go into a lot more detail about building rapport in Chapter 9.)

This is another thing that contributes to the Upward (or Downward) Spiral and is yet another reason why Public Speaking Monkey taming is so important for Mini Monkeys, not just Chunky Monkeys! Unfortunately, what might start out as a Mini Monkey, when reflected, can spiral out of control and project to many times its size!

## The meaning of all behaviour is contextual

Did you know that all behaviour is context dependant? I'd certainly never considered this before I learnt these more helpful mindsets. Said in another way, the 'meaning' will depend on the circumstances or background surrounding the behaviour. For example, at a regional meeting some jokes that are acceptable in the bar the night before may not be appropriate the next day in the meeting room. It isn't just controversial topics you need to be aware of – for example, amongst senior mangers it might be OK to challenge the CEO on their views, they may encourage it. But in a client meeting environment, that very same behaviour may not be OK.

There is research to show that people high on the autism

spectrum can suffer from 'context blindness', and with Aspergers sometimes undiagnosed in adults, bear in mind it is quite possible that people in your workplace may be on the spectrum, and unaware.

Ensure that your content, and that of your teams, is appropriate for the context such as the sector, division or country. Avoid rolling out the same old slide deck each time!

### *Jaffagate – Is a Jaffa Cake a cake or a biscuit?'*

For those of you not from the UK, and who haven't had the pleasure of consuming lots of Jaffa Cakes, they are a biscuit-sized sweet snack – with 3 yummy layers – a sponge base, a layer of orange flavoured jelly and a coating of chocolate.

I invite you, before you read on, to spend a few moments thinking about how you would answer the following question if you were in a job interview for a director level role:

*'Is a Jaffa Cake a cake or a biscuit?'*

I heard a story about a senior director who had this very question in their interview. The chap going for the interview said his response was to immediately say, *'It's a cake'*, and he went on to justify that view point. His mindset did not even entertain that there could be any opposing arguments or other views. He thought the interviewers were looking for certainty from a director.

He didn't get offered that role and it may or may not have been because of 'Jaffagate'. My view is that only a certain type of company, with a specific set of values would find that blinkered thinking appealing. Most senior leaders we work with are looking for the candidates to see a variety of contextual points of view, and then make a balanced decision.

Having worked in the biscuit industry myself, I remembered Her Majesty's Revenue and Customs have made 2 investigations into this matter, because if Jaffa Cakes were a cake, no VAT (Value Added Tax) would have to be paid on them, and if they were a biscuit (with chocolate) then VAT would need to be paid! The table shows some points that Her Majesty's Revenue and Customs used to make their decision.

| Points for a Jaffa Cake being a cake | Points for a Jaffa Cake being a biscuit |
|---|---|
| The product's name was a minor consideration | Size: Jaffa Cakes were in size more like biscuits than cakes |
| Cake would be expected to be soft and friable; biscuit would be expected to be crisp and able to be snapped. Jaffa Cakes had the texture of sponge cake | Marketing: Jaffa Cakes were generally displayed for sale with biscuits rather than cakes |
| On going stale, a Jaffa Cake goes hard like a cake rather than soft like a biscuit | Jaffa Cakes are presented as a snack, eaten with the fingers, whereas a cake may be more often expected to be eaten with a fork |
| The sponge part of a Jaffa Cake is a substantial part of the product in terms of bulk and texture when eaten | They also appeal to children, who could eat one in a few mouthfuls rather like a sweet. |
| Ingredients: cake can be made of widely differing ingredients, but Jaffa Cakes were made of an egg, flour, and sugar mixture which was aerated on cooking and was the same as a traditional sponge cake. It was a thin batter rather than the thicker dough expected for a biscuit texture | Packaging: Jaffa Cakes were sold in packages more similar to biscuits than cakes |

Taking all these factors in the table into account, it was ruled Jaffa Cakes had characteristics of both cakes and biscuits, but the tribunal thought they had enough characteristics of cakes to be accepted as such, and they therefore didn't have to pay VAT. So, in the context of the law, yes, they are cakes. But as we can see, when the context is changed to size, packaging, marketing, eating occasion and the buyer you'd have to visit if you were selling Jaffa Cakes, then depending on the context they may well be a biscuit!

Do you ever get annoyed or upset by feedback, comments or questions? If so, keep the 'context' in mind; with so many different backgrounds and cultures in the workplace today it is pretty tricky to assume that everyone will get exactly the right meaning in all sorts of contexts. So before jumping in and assuming the other person is wrong or rude, spend a few moments to see if, in fact, that communication would have been OK in a different context, and move on from there.

You'll find plenty more techniques for dealing with 'awkward' questions in Chapter 11. Next let's look at some next steps to work with these career-enhancing mindsets.

## Time to take action

### Being prepared exercise

1) Notice if you have the school of thought that everything must be 'perfect' on the day. There is a whole argument as to what perfect is anyway – but that's in my previous book. In fact, I think it's important to know that it may not go perfectly on the day.

2) Get ready to handle anything that happens and not be worried by it. Assuming your monkeys are 'Tamed', and you have the career-enhancing mindsets discussed then a wise thing to do is create your own list of things that could go wrong. Your list may look a little like this:

- Equipment doesn't work, breaks or is incompatible.
- You/audience member is in the wrong room.
- Not enough chairs.
- Trip over a wire (I've seen this – the chap was OK but had been speaking on health and safety - doh!)
- Someone walks out – for a bathroom break.
- There's a power cut or fire alarm.
- Timings aren't to plan – often overrunning.
- Refreshments don't arrive on time.
- Participants knowledge levels are not as predicted.
- Phone/text pings.
- People start texting/emailing.

3) For each item on the list write down how you might handle them. Then you'll be prepared, or at least less surprised!

## Practising High Performance Mindsets exercise

1) If you're ready to take action on improving your mindsets, awareness of the current and desired mindsets is a great first step. Identify where you have gaps and work on those.

2) Next, find opportunities to practise your new mindsets. Most of the mindsets discussed here apply to all conversations and communications, not just presentations. And that's good news because you can practise those concepts outside of the boardroom.

3) It doesn't need to be an overnight, instant success; it can be a gradual, continual improvement.

4) You might practise your new mindset in what you consider safer areas first – perhaps in a social context – then see the success it brings and as you gain confidence, you can bring the new approach into your work communications.

5) After improving your own mindsets, take a look at your team and see who else would benefit from improving their mindsets.

6) Decide how best to approach this and buy them this book!

## Wrapping up on growth mindset

Rarely do people manage their own mindset (and even if you do, some of your team may not). People with unmanaged mindsets run the risk of letting the external environment rule whether they feel good or bad. That may be someone coming back from a presentation and saying, *'They (the audience) were in a bad mood today'* or, *'Well what do you expect, I was given the graveyard slot'*. With the blame firmly with other people, the individual has less control over creating the results they want.

For those who use or take on board these mindsets, you may begin to feel that that it is only *you* who is in charge. You and your mindset decide how you feel, your responses to situations and therefore ultimately the results you get. You may not believe this yet and that's OK, but keep an open mind, experiment with the techniques and see what happens!

## *Adopting Helpful Monkeys*

A Public Speaking Monkey is made of two parts – the belief and the habits. Once a monkey has been 'Tamed', the negative belief either disappears or it is 'Tamed down' to a genuine Green Monkey. For example, if your old Red Monkey used to be *'I'm Not Good Enough'* then now it's 'Tamed', you won't believe that any more. Belief change might take some time to get to the point where it happens, but when it happens it is instantaneous. The bad habit side can take a little longer to disappear. Let's say you have been over-talking because of a *'You're Stupid'* Monkey – to break that habit takes practice. It will be easier as you no longer have the negative belief fuelling the bad habit, but it will need practice and review; it might not miraculously disappear immediately.

When thinking about presenting you may still have that old monkey voice pop into your head. The difference is that now you've 'Tamed' it, you have the power to change what the monkey voices say – so you can replace them with something more positive, a Helpful Monkey like, *'I'm a calm, confident and clear speaker'*. This takes some practice, but you've taken away the fuel from the fire – you now have choices. It's a bit like when people lose weight, they still try to wear their old baggy 'favourite' clothes, but after a few wears they realise those old clothes don't fit their new selves (literally) and don't fit the new image of themselves they are beginning to see.

You must be able to believe the Helpful Monkey statement you've created – you can't bully your monkey into submission; this will only lead to stress and trouble later down the line. So, if *'I'm a calm, confident and clear speaker'* is too much of a stretch to believe at the point in time when you've only just 'Tamed' your monkeys, then you could start with, *'I'm becoming a calm, confident and clear speaker'* or *'It's going to be OK'*.

My first book shows you step by step how to 'Tame' those pesky Public Speaking Monkeys. There is also information on our website, www.SimplyAmazingTraining.co.uk.

## *Staying on the Upward Spiral*

The Upward Spiral is the opposite of the Downward Spiral, and if there was a silver bullet to mindsets, this would be it: your aim is to continually strive to stay on the Upward Spiral.

### What does the Upward spiral look like?

The Upward Spiral doesn't have to start at any amazingly positive place. It can begin with a Helpful Monkey belief as tiny as *'I'm OK'* or *'it's going to be OK'*. As long as it is (even a little bit) positive, then the spiral itself will lift you up from there so that over time you'll be giving engaging, persuasive and inspiring presentations.

Once we tell ourselves, *'It's going to be OK'* what happens then? Now our mind can begin to work, instead of focussing on a block. You can ensure you prepare and follow my tips. You can feel confident knowing you know your material because you've practised it and it went well. You can, nearer the time, ensure you physically prepare well – get a good night's sleep the day before, arrive early and check out your environment.

## Good Presentation

- good feedback
- answer questions easily
- adapt as required
- audience engaged
- speak confidently
- breath calmly
- positive body language
- good eye contact
- audience feels comfortable
- smile and relax
- feel good
- sleep well
- practise material
- prepare SAS

(Helpful Monkey)

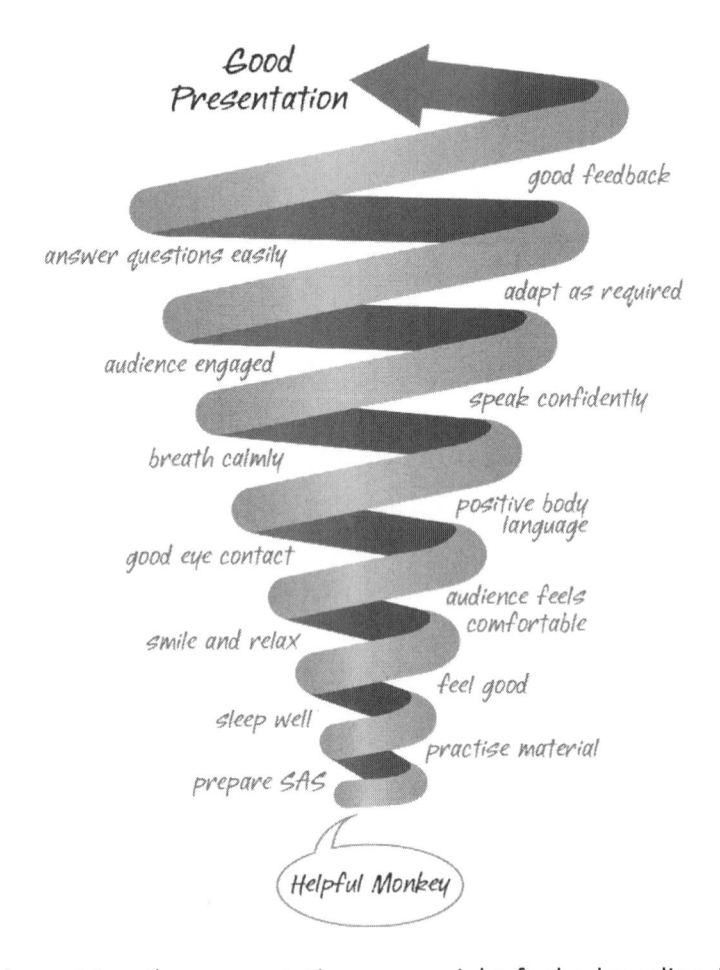

Before giving the presentation, you might feel adrenaline (like butterflies in your stomach) and that's natural if it is an important presentation, but with your monkeys 'Tamed' you'll no longer feel nerves (negative voices/feeling). Like an athlete before a race, they may say they were pumped with adrenaline, but they wouldn't say they were nervous.

## Body language and the Upward Spiral

When you are about to give the presentation, the spiral is equally powerful – if you are thinking, *'I'm going to be OK'*, then your body language will be more positive as you come into the room. Most people think body language is only about looking good, but good body language impacts you and your audience:

A. You'll be able to hold your head high which:
   i. Allows you to breathe easily as you've not blocked off half your throat.
   ii. Portrays confidence to the audience.
   iii. Gives you a feeling of confidence.
B. You'll be able to smile which:
   i. Helps you build rapport, so the audience begin to like you.
   ii. Makes the audience feel relaxed, so they open up.
   iii. Unconsciously encourages the audience to smile back at you.
C. You will stand upright with your back straight and shoulders back which means:
   i. You can project your voice and speak clearly without shouting.
   ii. You will look taller and more authoritative, so the audience will more likely want to listen.
   iii. You feel secure, rooted and not light headed.

There's more on body language in Chapter 10. For now, know that as your body language improves, so does your confidence. And as your confidence improves, so does your mindset, your ability to remember everything you practised and so on – they are all interconnected. They are all parts of you that contribute to High Performance Presentations.

Can body language come before mindset? You may be

wondering why I'm insistent that mindset has to come first if these things are all connected. Surely you could start with your body language and then go from there? Well sort of. Yes, short term if you can practise good body language and breathe correctly and so on then you will begin to feel better, but if the monkey is still there, you'll be having a mini argument in your head whilst presenting. *'I'm OK, no wait I'm not, how can I be because I'm stupid!',* and so on. Whilst you are having this tug of war in your mind, there is no room to concentrate on the audience and what they want. (*'Oh yes! I forgot there was an audience watching!'*) So, the chance of slipping back onto the Downward Spiral is increasing by the second.

## But is it possible to stay on the Upward Spiral forever?

Clients often at this point also wonder if it is possible to stay on the Upward Spiral forever and I think it is. Avoid pressurising yourself to have to do that. Even if you slip off a few times onto the Downward Spiral, you will catch yourself early and be able to stop the decline using some of the specific tips from later in the book. These techniques will take you quickly back to the Upward Spiral, and you'll start to go up again. It's very empowering to know that you can regain control and re-switch to the Upward Spiral.

## Upward Spiral exercise

1) If you want to experience the Upward Spiral body language for yourself, try each of the points described in A,B & C above. Move your body into that position, notice the new more positive feelings and imagine the audience's reactions to them.

2) Of course, it won't *feel* natural yet (the body language that

*feels* natural to westerners tends to be hunched up over a laptop!) That will come with practice, but open your mind enough to see how it feels once you are past the *'it's not natural'* thing – because actually it is perfectly natural. This is how nature intended us to be!

3) You will need to practise this new positive body language until it becomes second nature – and you can practise it almost everywhere and you'll begin to see the benefits are huge.

## What next?

Now we've covered mindsets, it's time to look at presentation toolsets and skillsets. From now on in the book, the Presenter Personality Style preferences are used to help guide you to potential areas of strength and weakness, so you can create your own prioritised plan of action to ensure you deliver engaging, persuasive and inspiring High Performance Presentations.

# Chapter 6
# Prepare for the Simply Amazing Structure™ (SAS)

The first toolset essential in creating High Performance Presentations is basic but often overlooked – audience preparation. Then we'll move on to starting to see what the Simply Amazing Structure (SAS) looks like.

## *Audience preparation*

### Why audience understanding is essential

All High Performance Presentations consider the audience and what they want. But the majority of business professionals I train admit to not thinking much (if at all) about the audience during the planning process.

**Low Performance Presentation warning!**

Rarely do people begin their presentation planning with the end in mind. Even if they do, it's often not the most helpful end goal they are aiming for. A less helpful end goal might be:

- ✗ *'I hope the presentation is over soon, so I can sit down.'*
- ✗ *'I hope they will see how hard I/my team have been working on this project.'*
- ✗ *'They need to see that my way is THE way forward.'*

When I hear this in my coaching sessions I say, *'The presentation isn't about you, it is about the audience. Otherwise you may as well just speak to the mirror!'*

That's not to say that you don't have an agenda – but that should be positively positioned and blended with the needs of the audience. If you want to communicate in a successful, persuasive manner that inspires action, then the audience should never feel that your agenda is higher than theirs! This links back to the push vs. pull concept mentioned in Chapter 1.

> **The presentation ISN'T about you –
> it is about the audience**

High Performance Presentations consider the audience, their needs and wants, and are planned accordingly.

## What do you need to know about the audience?

The first key consideration in preparing a presentation is to consider the audience. To do that you need to know who they are. Sounds obvious right? Later there are 3 exercises to show you exactly how to do that.

**Low Performance Presentation warning!**

A sure-fire way to give a Low Performance Presentation is to just talk about your agenda with no regard to the audience. Avoid recycling the same presentation deck and droning on about things that aren't relevant to the audience. The audience won't say anything – but therein lies the danger as you continue to do it again and again.

Let's take a quick look at your potential personality style in this area, so you can bear that in mind as you read through:

> **Sociable**
>
> Your flexibility means you should find it relatively easy to adapt to the needs of the audience (once you put in the time and energy).

> **Caring**
>
> Your strength in people means you may well find it relatively easy to understand the needs of the audience and adapt accordingly (make sure you aren't being too flexible though).

> **Information**
>
> Because you are so thorough you'll be able to work through these exercises each time you present to the appropriate level (make sure you keep it big picture and adapt as needed).

> **Results**
>
> You are quick to decide, so once you know the improved results that will come from this approach you can use it frequently. (Ensure you slow down enough to see the benefits shine through.)

To give consistently High Performance Presentations, you need to be part chameleon and consider the audience's styles that aren't the same as yours. They digest information differently so make sure you adapt your style to give them what they want in the way they want it.

For example, if the <u>audience</u> is:

1. **Results** preference, they like to know immediate options and consequences and are most comfortable with a fast tempo.

2. **Sociable** preference, they like to interact at high speed and with variety. They become bored with details and enjoy constantly changing direction. They will enjoy interactive exercises.

3. **Caring** preference, you will need to demonstrate that you are caring, trustworthy and open. You need to show that you can support them in their personal needs and those of their team.

4. **Information** preference, they will be won over by orderliness, accuracy, persistence and follow through, so ensure that you use data, facts and quotations to support your presentation. Exact numbers, facts, spelling, grammar and even punctuation are all important here.

## How to understand your audience more

You may already have your own techniques and if they are working, great! Keep them. If you don't already do much audience preparation, like most people, then consider working through these exercises. Let's get going!

I've listed some thought-provoking audience questions below. Making notes as you go through these, with your next presentation in mind, will help you to experience the value of these questions, so grab a pen!

## Audience preparation exercise 1

1. Who are the audience? (For example, team members, employees, agencies, board members, factory workers, accountants, salespeople, investors, conference delegates, bankers, shoppers, mums, sportspeople, business owners, church goers.)
2. Consider if there is likely to be a preference or dominance in one or two of the Presenter Personality Styles in the audience, for example, systems teams may have more of an **Information** bias.
3. Imagine you are a typical audience member, give yourself a representative name and persona e.g. Julie from Marketing. Then ask yourself:
    a. Why do I want to spend my time listening to this presentation? What will I gain? What are the many ways in which I will benefit from listening?
    b. What do I want from this presentation? Or what do I want to hear from this presenter?
    c. What preconceived ideas might I be bringing to this presentation?
    d. What are my emotions, hopes and fears? (Make sure you consider these in your communications.)
    e. What is my mindset in relation to this topic?

    f. What information do I need to see/hear/feel in order to make a decision, be persuaded or take action?

    g. What are all the objections I might have (large and small)? – For example, *'it won't work'*, *'it costs too much'* or *'we tried it before'*).

    h. How will you persuade me through facts? (Case studies and market research are a great way to demonstrate your believability.)

    i. How do you realistically want me to action this information after the presentation?

    j. What communication would it be best to do before the meeting or presentation?

If there are different groups in the audience with different needs (like finance in addition to marketing) then you need to create a persona per group, e.g. Fred from Finance, and answer the questions above for each and every persona.

## Audience preparation exercise 2 (advanced)

1) A more in-depth exercise, (adapted from Darren Hardy), if you really want to get under the audience's skin for an important presentation, is to imagine you are a typical audience member (like Julie or Fred) lying in bed staring at the ceiling.

2) Now imagine those few moments before you fall asleep where you might be reviewing the challenges of the day … or those few moments when you first wake up and you are considering the objectives and hopes of the day ahead, and ask yourself the questions below:

- What am I thinking about?

- What am I worried about?
- Who am I worried about?
- What do I fear?
- Who do I fear?
- What do I hope for?
- Who do I hope to impress?
- What are my desires, ambitions and goals?
- What do I think I need help with?
- What resources, ideas or assistance am I looking for to overcome my unspoken fears or accomplish my innermost desires?

3) Later you'll be able to see where you can use these deeper insights into the audience's mind to help you improve your presentation preparation.

## Audience preparation exercise 3

Finally, it's time to understand how you want to make your audience feel. Your big picture goal for them. Complete the following exercise:

1) Make a list of one-word answers to the question, *'What is important to me about how the audience feel after the presentation?'* for example, is it about:

- ✓ Buy-in.
- ✓ Change.
- ✓ Confidence.

2) Once you have your list, spend a few moments putting the words in order so you can see what is most and least important for them to feel. When I do this with my clients they often uncover some interesting insights. Did you?

3) Refer back to this list if you feel you might be getting sidetracked at any stage of the presentation creation.

## Wrap up

If you don't consider your audience first, your presentation will be like so many others that you listen to – the audience could get bored or frustrated. When you consider the audience and adapt to their needs, the talk becomes engaging and interesting almost before you begin!

> **Avoid being the one who recycles the same presentation deck they did last year and drones on about things that aren't relevant to the audience.**

With the audience preparation firmly in mind, let's look at the structure of the presentation, and the second toolset, the Simply Amazing Structure™ (SAS). The individual elements of the SAS are in the next chapter – before that, let's look at some background and foundations to the SAS.

## *Why is structure the bedrock for success?*

The structure of a presentation or talk is really important. It lays the foundations upon which everything else is built. By presenting information in an easy-to-understand structure (the SAS) you'll see much more success. The fact that you have all the right 'bits' doesn't mean you have a compelling presentation! If you don't present them in an appropriate order, your talk can be at best confusing and at worst rejected or ignored.

With a well-planned structure, not only will you be sharing the information in an easily digestible manner – you'll also be able to see if there are any missing pieces of information from the 'jigsaw puzzle'.

By creating an easy-to-follow structure, you, as the presenter will be able to remember it more easily because it follows a logical thread and a story. We often work with people who tell us they have a 'terrible memory' and they'll 'never remember what to say'. But once they've spent the time working out a good strong SAS they know it, almost off by heart, before we even ask them to 'learn' it (we'll show you how to visually learn your key points later in Chapter 8).

## The SAS in relation to Presenter Personality Styles

As you create your first SAS you may naturally find some sections less easy than others and that's OK – it probably means that section isn't your preferred style. All the more reason to practise it then! All styles benefit from using the SAS and remember you are a blend of all the types; but in order to help you, see some potential blind spots generalised below:

*Sociable*

Because structure and planning are low in your natural style you would benefit from paying attention to some sort of structure! Using the Simply Amazing Structure™ will allow you enough freedom to play to your strengths of incorporating some ad lib and adapting to those in the room, yet provide a framework to help the audience follow your message and allow you to finish on time! You are likely to enjoy the WHAT IF section so pay particular attention to providing enough information, especially in the WHAT and being specific about next steps in the HOW section.

*Caring*

Using the SAS will allow you to ensure you give the audience what they want in a way that they understand it. Your strength of reading people well will help with the WHY section and the rest of the structure. You might want to pay particular attention to the HOW section in clearly signalling the next steps and bringing other people's actions to a close (it may feel a bit too directive for you until you get used to it). You may also want to practise communicating in a more concise manner, especially in the WHAT section, for an extraverted preference audience, and this structure will help you do that.

### *Information*

Structure and planning is your strength and you'll have all the right details for the WHAT sections. But you might need to watch out not to overdo the preparation and not to put in too much detail or some of the other styles may get bored and lost along the way. The SAS helps you consider the audience, so it will ensure you only include what the audience needs, not everything you want to tell them. You'll enjoy this because it gives you a structure to use every time, in almost all communication contexts, to design the communication and sift through what is and isn't needed in the SAS, especially the WHAT section.

### **Results**

Getting action is your strength so you may find the HOW section easier – just ensure you know silence from more introverted preference styles required more in-depth understanding. You might benefit from ensuring you always consider the WHY and WHAT from the audience's perspective and generally you'd benefit from pacing the audience more appropriately – perhaps check in with a more introverted preference colleague to get feedback on your pace. More about pacing later in Chapter 9.

## *SAS – Background and foundations*

### Where did SAS come from?

Since learning the 4MAT® learning styles concept by Bernice McCarthy (world-renowned educational theorist) I've used it as an excellent foundation to my presentation structure. Over the years I've built on it to create the Simply Amazing Structure™ (SAS) and I use this for important communications – including writing this book! I encourage clients to use it too because of its simplicity and flexibility. Like anything, it's easy once you've learnt it! The SAS means the audience (with all different styles) get what they need and want from your communication.

### Using mind maps for preparation

There are many preparation techniques. Mind mapping initially and then using the SAS works well for most people. There is plenty of information on mind mapping on the web and I highly recommend you discover more. I find mind mapping especially useful if I'm ever stuck for a place to start. Sometimes I find a topic or project can be so overwhelming that just putting everything down on paper, in no specific order on a visual mind map, is a great place to begin.

Write the core topic in the centre and add thoughts and ideas from the start of each branch; then related ideas or concepts attach to relevant branches and so on as illustrated below.

If you already know your topic, or once the mind map takes form, move the content into the SAS. For most presentations SAS is where I start because I know my topic well – as do you, especially if you've been in your role or business for some time.

# HIGH PERFORMANCE PRESENTATIONS

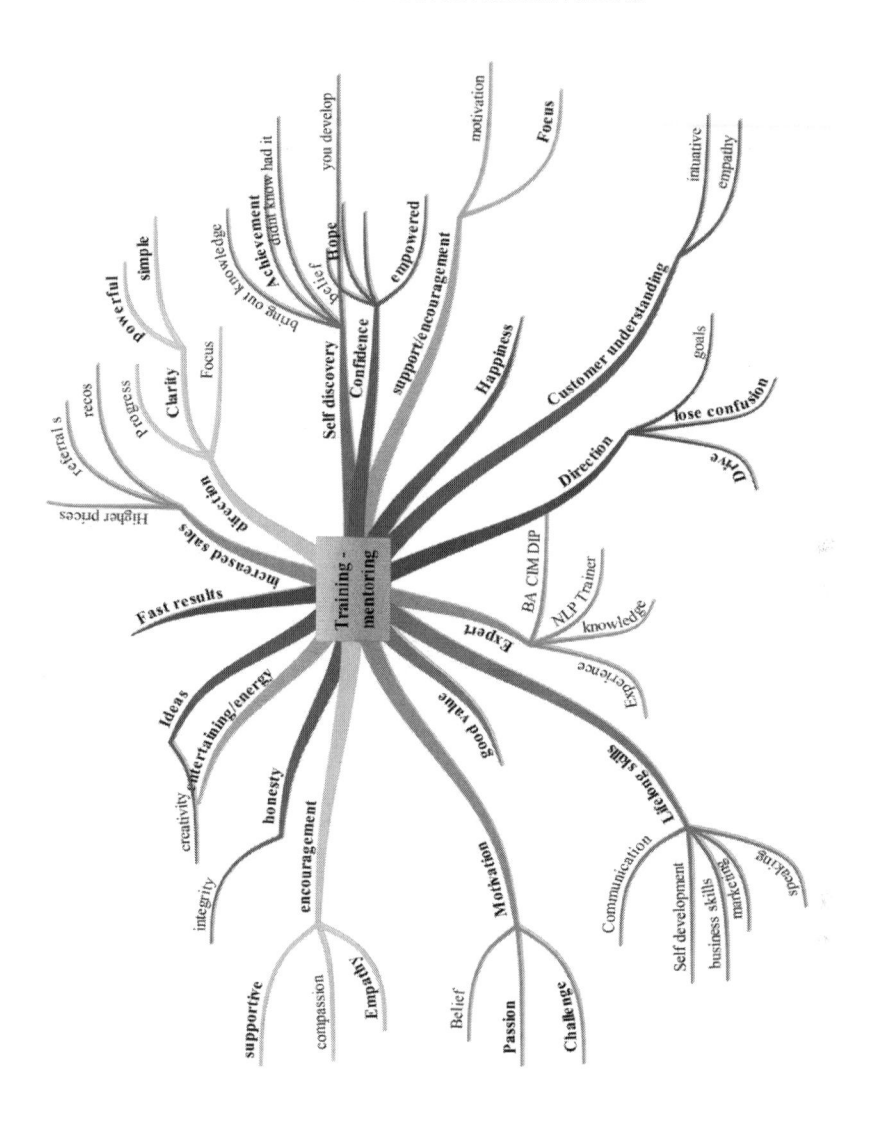

The best way to work with SAS

**Pen and paper**

Let me take a minute to talk about how to best organise your ideas. Pen and paper!

'What?' I hear you cry. You thought I was going to tell you

about the latest gadget – but gadgets are partly to blame for Low Performance Presentations. Do not prepare on computer and especially not on PowerPoint.

If you're asked to give a presentation, do you haul out the laptop, open up PowerPoint and then stare blankly at the screen. Ring any bells? Do you spend the first 30 minutes deciding on the title slide and the font?!

## Three is the magic number

This is one of the oldest of all the presentation toolsets, known about since the time of Aristotle (he wrote about it in his book 'Rhetoric'). People tend to remember things in threes, so when you structure your presentation around threes it will become more memorable for you and the audience.

Lists or sets of three are also very memorable:

1. **'Friends, Romans, Countrymen** *lend me your ears'* – *William Shakespeare.*
2. **'Stop, look and listen'** – Public safety announcement.
3. **'Yes we can!** '– Barack Obama's presidential campaign.

A classic example of the magic number was Winston Churchill's famous Blood, Sweat and Tears speech. He is widely attributed as saying, 'I can promise you nothing but blood, sweat and tears'. What he actually said was, 'I can promise you blood, sweat, toil and tears' and because of the rule of three, it has been remembered in history as 'blood, sweat and tears'.

If you are of a certain age you may remember the 1990 song by De La Soul, 'Magic Number'. Whilst I'm not sure it is to my musical taste, it is very memorable!

Keep the magic number in mind as you learn more about engaging, persuasive and inspiring presentations.

## SAS Template

Before we go into each of these sections in more detail, spend a moment looking at the whole structure of the SAS. The grid illustrated below moves in a clockwise direction – LITTLE INTROduction, WHY, WHAT, HOW, WHAT IF.

```
                    | Little Intro |
     What if?       |    Why?
                    |
       Q&T          |     ✓
                    |
       - ve         |     ✓
                    |
       + ve         |     ✓
    _____|_____
       How?         |    What?
        1           |     ┌────
        2           |     │────
        3           |     
     - - - - - - - -|     ┌────
        4           |     │────
        5           |     
        6           |     ┌────
        7           |     │────
```

The visuals are three ticks for WHY, 3 rectangles or boxes with 3 branches coming from each rectangle for the WHAT, number 1 to 7 for the HOW (with a dotted line between 3 and 4, and the letters Q & T followed by a negative sign (-ve) and a positive sign (+ve) for the WHAT IF section).

## SAS case study exercise

It will be useful as you go through the next section to have an example of your own to think about.

1. If you have a presentation coming up, work with that.
2. Otherwise, come up with something you might like to,

or might be asked to speak about, and keep it in mind as we go through the content.
3. Once we've discussed the structure, there are exercises for you to do on your own case study example.
4. Wait until the exercises are written out to start on your own version of each section, because there's a bit of a twist to the order of preparation as you'll discover later.

## SAS template exercise

1. Copy the SAS template above onto a blank page.
2. Keep to the visuals shown. This will help later when it comes to easily remembering the SAS and knowing what you want to say.
3. Later, you'll get to fill it in with your example presentation.

### *Low Performance Presentation warning!*

To avoid Low Performance Presentations don't prepare on a PC! That moves your mind into detail mode. When we type we are programmed to think about fonts, spelling and the detail, not the big picture. When I say draw it out, I mean it! Use a pen and paper which allows the unconscious mind to think freely.

Now we're ready to look at each of the sections of the SAS.

# HIGH PERFORMANCE PRESENTATIONS

# Chapter 7
# Create Your Simply Amazing Structure™ (SAS)

Although in this context you'll be using the SAS for presenting, you can use it in the future for anything – websites, leaflets, emails, letters, etc. That's great news in itself, because it means you don't have to wait until you next present to practise it. You can get going on your next important email!

When you use SAS the audience will:

- ✓ Feel comfortable and be able to follow what you are saying in an easy-to-digest manner.
- ✓ Understand the information's usefulness now and in the future.
- ✓ Feel it is personalised, and thus be engaged, because they have their communication style/needs addressed.

You as a presenter will:

- ✓ Know where you are going at all times and know why you are communicating each section.
- ✓ Feel confident and thus exude executive presence and make the audience feel confident.
- ✓ Know you've prepared well and covered all the key points and are ready for any questions and feedback.

## *The elements of SAS*

Here are the sections of the SAS:

- ✓ Beginning
    - ◆ LITTLE INTROduction – Deliver a short introduction; no more than a few sentences.
    - ◆ WHY – Give your audience three reasons why they would want to listen to your talk.
- ✓ Middle
    - ◆ WHAT – Share the actual content, facts and information of your talk.
    - ◆ HOW – Explain how the audience can use or action the information you have shared.
- ✓ End
    - ◆ WHAT IF – Allow ample time for the audience to ask questions, reflect and then wrap-up.

This SAS is specifically designed to ensure the best possible engagement from your audience. It is important to realise that using the SAS forces you to think about the audience and not yourself. The structure is created from a collection of the basic questions any **audience member** might have in mind:

1. What are we talking about, big picture?
2. Why do I want to listen to this?
3. What facts, information and data do I need to know?
4. How is this relevant and significant for me, right now?
5. What if I want to adapt or build on this in the future in some way?

The more you plan your presentation in advance and spend

time considering how the audience will listen to the information, the more success you will see. This SAS is an iterative process, which means that you build on it, go back and forth until it is right. You shouldn't expect perfection first time, and to do that will only hinder you. Go for it, make a good effort and then later be OK knowing you'll change it as you go forwards and backwards. That's the process and that's OK, and believe it or not, you will also save yourself a lot of time in the long run. I'll explain more about that later.

## Beginning – The LITTLE INTROduction and the WHY

### The LITTLE INTROduction

Firstly, you need to set the scene with a short and snappy introduction, which I call the LITTLE INTRO. Of course. we want to hear who you are and what you're speaking about but please, avoid telling us where you went to school or what you had for breakfast! Just a short introduction will suffice – a few sentences maximum. The aim of this introduction is threefold: to build rapport with the audience, to begin to build credibility with the audience if necessary, and to ensure they know the context of the talk or presentation. Allow for the fact that some of the audience may not have read any invitations or pre-material in any detail and, of course, their minds might be elsewhere. This will ensure all of the audience are on the same page when you begin.

### Low Performance Presentation warning!

Many presentations start off with a 10-minute section on the speaker personally or their company and why they're so amazing. Boring! Personally, I come from the, *'I'll think you're amazing when you get on with it and tell me something I'm interested in'* school of thought! That said, you do need to have built enough credibility for them to begin to listen to you. Strike an appropriate balance.

### The WHY section

This section answers the first question the audience member is asking: WHY? *'Why would I want to listen to this talk?'* The audience then knows why they want to engage fully and listen. The intention is to give three audience motivators.

Time-wise the WHY section isn't long, but it is important.

In my day (don't you just love that phrase? I wonder at what age you can start using that?) I rarely learnt or understood how what I was learning would be useful in real life. I had no idea why I had to learn about Roman roads for example. What use would that ever be to me (even though I since lived in the old Roman city of St Albans for 12 years)?

Having used this very example in a presentation skills training to PhD students and university lecturers, a participant very quickly told me that Roman roads were straight (I knew that bit) which meant that if I wanted to get somewhere more quickly, all other things being equal, a Roman road would be faster! Well I never thought of that!

The point I'm making is rarely did lessons get related in the short term to real-life implications. As I write this book, Finland have just announced 'Phenomenal' teaching – teaching by topics, e.g. studying 'Working in a café', and through that you'll learn Maths, English, Home Economics, etc. Hopefully this will catch on.

**Low Performance Presentation warning!**

If you can't think of any WHYs, change the talk. It's your role to give the audience reasons to listen and clearly demonstrate what they'll gain by listening. If the audience have been told to come to the talk it's even more important to cover this bit well. They may have been 'told' to turn up, however, no one but you can encourage them to listen and be persuaded.

## Example WHYs

WHYs can be either 'positive' motivations (like increase or improve) or 'negative' motivations (like avoid or reduce) or a mix of both. Note: negatives can be motivating as some people tend to prefer to move away from pain rather than towards gain. A mix is often a good idea.

To help you, here are some examples of some WHYs:

| 'Positive' Motivators | 'Negative' Motivators |
|---|---|
| ✓ Build confidence | ✓ Lose fear |
| ✓ Grow sales | ✓ Save money |
| ✓ Create time | ✓ Save time |
| ✓ Improve life | ✓ Reduce hassle |
| ✓ Hit target | ✓ Miss target |
| ✓ Make bonus | ✓ Lose bonus |
| ✓ Motivate team | ✓ De-motivate team |
| ✓ Increase efficiency | ✓ Reduce waste |
| ✓ Keep safe | ✓ Save lives |

## WHY SAS exercise

1. Imagine you're an audience member (e.g. Fred in Finance) and list as many reasons as you can think of in answer to the question *'Why would I want to listen to*

*this talk?'* Go ahead and do this now for your case study example presentation.
2. Narrow this long list down to your top 3 for this specific audience. Note: Keep hold of the other ideas as you may change your mind later or want to use those in another talk with a different audience.
3. Summarise each of your top 3 WHYs into:
    a. Two key words – before you ask, no, that doesn't mean when you say it out loud you'll only say two words; it just means these two words will act as your aide memoires.
    b. The first word needs to suggest movement and action (e.g. increase, prevent, share, save) and the second word will be the subject you are talking about (e.g. sales, accidents, success, money). Following this rule will ensure you avoid the common mistake of straying prematurely into the WHAT section and keep you firmly in the WHY section.
    c. Check your balance of positive and negative WHYs is appropriate for your audience.
    d. Finally, decide what order would suit the audience best.
4. Now choose your top three audience motivators and pop them into your SAS template as shown. This is an iterative process. I would expect you to revisit this in due course so 80–90% there is good enough for now.

```
                    ┌──────────────┐
                    │ Little Intro │
                    └──────────────┘
   What if?           │  Why?
                      │
    Q&T               │  ✓ Save Time
                      │
    - ve              │  ✓ Hit Target
                      │
    + ve              │  ✓ Improve Efficiency
   ─────────────────────────────────────
    How?              │  What?
    1                 │   ┌──┐
    2                 │   │  │──
                      │   └──┘
    3                 │
    4                 │   ┌──┐
                      │   │  │──
    5                 │   └──┘
    6                 │   ┌──┐
                      │   │  │──
    7                 │   └──┘
```

Some people are very good at understanding and empathizing with what others want, and typically **Results** and **Information** preferences may find it less easy. If you find it not so easy, then practise really getting under the skin of a specific representative audience member like Fred or Julie. Use your audience preparation answers from Chapter 6 to help you, or ask other people, e.g. colleagues, who could represent your audience well.

## Low Performance Presentation warning!

Avoid jumping straight into the content without motivating people to listen with your 3 WHYs first. If you do you risk the audience sitting there thinking, *'Why am I wasting my time listening to this?'* – or worse still, checking their emails on their phones!

### *Two case studies*

We will follow two case studies: the SAS for a weight loss product and the SAS for a presentation skills training course. I've chosen the diet product because I feel that almost everyone reading this book will know what I mean and be able to associate with it. I want you to imagine those ads on TV or in magazines that promise a wonderful solution to someone being overweight. Then imagine you work for the diet product company and are presenting to an audience of interested potential consumers. The potential WHYs for the diet product are shown in the picture.

# HIGH PERFORMANCE PRESENTATIONS

| | Diet Product |
|---|---|
| **What if?** | **Why?** |
| Q&T | ✓ Lose Weight |
| − ve | ✓ Improve Health |
| + ve | ✓ Feel Confident |
| **How?** | **What?** |
| 1 | |
| 2 | |
| 3 | |
| 4 | |
| 5 | |
| 6 | |
| 7 | |

Now let's look at the second, more advanced case study of a presentation skills training course. Imagine for a moment that you work alongside me as a licensee, helping professionals improve their presentation skills. If you were presenting to a room of business people with mixed experience and interest in learning presentation skills, the potential WHYs need to work harder because not everyone in the room is motivated to listen yet.

Including both work and personal reasons can, depending on the context, work really well. For the presentation skills training case study, the WHY might be, 'This presentation will help you to lose your nerves by 'Taming' those pesky Public Speaking Monkeys. It will help you to communicate more clearly and for those of you with children, nieces and nephews, once you've learnt these skills you can pass them on to aid the younger, (face-to-face communication starved) generation, too.'

I might use this approach where some of the audience aren't in the type of role where they have to present or speak all that often, so the first two WHYs are less relevant for them — because they feel they can just avoid speaking situations. If they aren't totally motivated for career purposes, including one or more personal WHYs will help engage them, and the idea of helping others will mean that even if they aren't motivated for themselves, they might do it to help their children, nephews or nieces.

This is illustrated in the SAS template as follows:

# HIGH PERFORMANCE PRESENTATIONS

| | Presentation Skills |
|---|---|
| **What if?** | **Why?** |
| Q&T | ✓ Lose Nerves |
| − ve | ✓ Clearer Communication |
| + ve | ✓ Aid Younger |
| **How?** | **What?** |
| 1 | |
| 2 | |
| 3 | |
| 4 | |
| 5 | |
| 6 | |
| 7 | |

## Middle – The WHAT and the HOW

### The WHAT section

This is the answer to the audience's next question, *'What is this all about and what information do I need to know?'* The answer often forms the main element of the content, covering the facts and information, the data, and background perhaps.

Having a well-organised, flowing and clear WHAT section means the audience can follow your argument step by step, digest the information more easily and important points can stand out and be easily remembered.

*Organising the WHAT section*

To organise the WHAT section, use the magic number to divide it into three parts. There are two different ways to do this:

**Chronologically** – A story with a beginning, middle and end. In this case the chunks are generally best delivered in time order.

**Separately** – A presentation made of three, almost standalone, separate chunks. (I'm going to come back to this structure later – after the HOW section.)

For now, let's assume we have a chronologically organised presentation. In which case the three WHAT chunks could be:

WHAT 1 – Beginning

WHAT 2 – Middle

WHAT 3 – End

Next, depending on the length of the presentation and depth

of content, you will likely branch off each WHAT section into three, as illustrated in the following template.

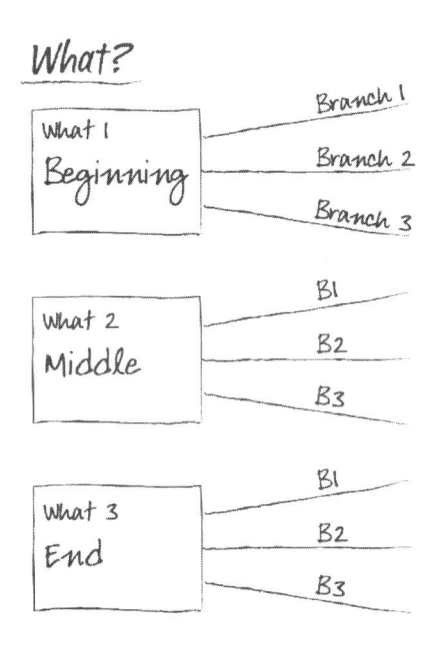

*What?*

```
┌─────────────┐──── Branch 1
│   What 1    │
│  Beginning  │──── Branch 2
│             │
└─────────────┘──── Branch 3

┌─────────────┐──── B1
│   What 2    │
│   Middle    │──── B2
│             │
└─────────────┘──── B3

┌─────────────┐──── B1
│   What 3    │
│    End      │──── B2
│             │
└─────────────┘──── B3
```

As a guide for a 20–60 minute presentation, I suggest having no more than three branches coming off each of the 3 WHATs.

### *What level of detail is needed in the WHAT?*

It is important to be able to move between the big picture and the detail appropriately in your presentation because:

- ✓ It is essential for structuring your presentation topics appropriately.
- ✓ It is necessary for tailoring messages to mixed audiences e.g. town hall meetings.
- ✓ It is the cornerstone of building rapport, pacing the audience (moving at the right speed for them) and even advanced question-answering techniques.

However, if you are an expert in your field, watch out because ironically your expertise may be holding you back from engaging, persuasive and inspiring presentations! At this stage of the preparation you need to think very top line and big picture, and some people don't find this easy at all – often **Information** and **Caring** personalities. Many of my clients are great in the detail and find it less easy to work at the level of big picture. My theory on why that might be is because of the classic education system and traditional career progression path.

Things may have changed a little now but when I went to school we learnt things by subject, and within that we learnt sub-subjects. Rarely was a big picture presented to us. For example, I do not remember being taught how mathematics was related in any way to the other subjects I was taking or jobs I might want in the future. I just learnt things mostly in silos and if I ever connected anything, that was through my own process, not those encouraged by the educational system. In geography I remember learning about the Brazilian rain forest, but I don't remember being encouraged to 'chunk up' that knowledge to apply it to weather patterns, culture or the environment in general.

Then there is the standard professional career path: you learn your craft, perhaps by taking more exams in specific subjects, e.g. solicitors, doctors, architects, engineers, accountants and so on. As you learn more, and specialise more, in an area you may get more and more rewarded and praised for your progress. But then comes that promotion to 'management' or some such level, where you are no longer expected to be in the detail. In fact, quite the opposite: the role is usually more about the bigger picture – it's about people, communication, influence and persuasion and seeing the trends – not managing the minutia.

The problem is 'they' often don't tell you this! It's like a secret code you are meant to understand. The skills that got you to this point can be less and less relevant. If it's not working well you try harder and harder to make it work, but you are still using the skills that worked before, when in fact you need new, different skills. That's what I believe contributes to the issue some people talk about of being 'promoted to incompetence'. It may not be significant enough to be noticed, but it may well be holding back your communications and possibly your career. The good news is that those skills can be learned if you know what they are.

*People on the autistic spectrum*

Another challenge is that people on the autistic spectrum, whilst all different, can (because of the way their brains work) have difficulties sorting things into categories. Someone on the spectrum might not naturally classify things easily, and therefore mightn't find it so easy to see the interconnectedness of things, or they may connect things in ways others might not see as 'obvious'.

For a more detailed explanation of this, see the excellent work by Temple Grandin – a high-functioning autistic woman who has made movies and books about her experiences. She says, *'Steve Jobs was probably mildly on the autistic spectrum. Basically, you've probably known people who were geeky and socially awkward but very smart. When does geeks and nerds become autism? That's a gray area. Half the people in Silicon Valley probably have autism.*' My out-take from learning more is that plenty of the clever people we work with, or present to, may well be on the spectrum without even realising it. If they are so high-functioning it is less likely to be identified.

From my limited experience of helping people with autism to 'chunk up' and put things into categories, you need to fully explain what *you* may consider to be obvious. For example, if you have given some big picture feedback on project 'A', e.g. *'Think of the customer's perspective more often'*, you need to expressly say that feedback applies to all projects going forward, e.g. project 'B', project 'C', project 'D' etc *and* to marketing you may be doing, and in emails and all communication.

*How to move between the big picture and the detail*

There is a simple, but perhaps under-appreciated tool called 'The Hierarchy Of Ideas' if you want to Google it. We can communicate at different levels – from detail to big picture or specific to global, by 'chunking down' or 'chunking up'. Let's look at life itself, and start with mammals, then let's assume we are using Google to help us discover more:

If you want more detail (to chunk down), what would you type into the Google search box to gain more detail on mammals? Perhaps *'examples of mammals'* or *'types of mammal'*.

If you wanted to go bigger picture (chunk up), higher than mammals, what would you type into Google? Perhaps: *'What is mammal an example of?' 'What family is mammal a part of?'* If you kept asking Google those bigger picture or chunking up questions you'd be highly likely to eventually arrive at 'Life'.

You can move up and down in the Hierarchy Of Ideas by imagining that you are Google, and ensuring you enter the right search sentence. Below is a visual illustration of the Hierarchy Of Ideas.

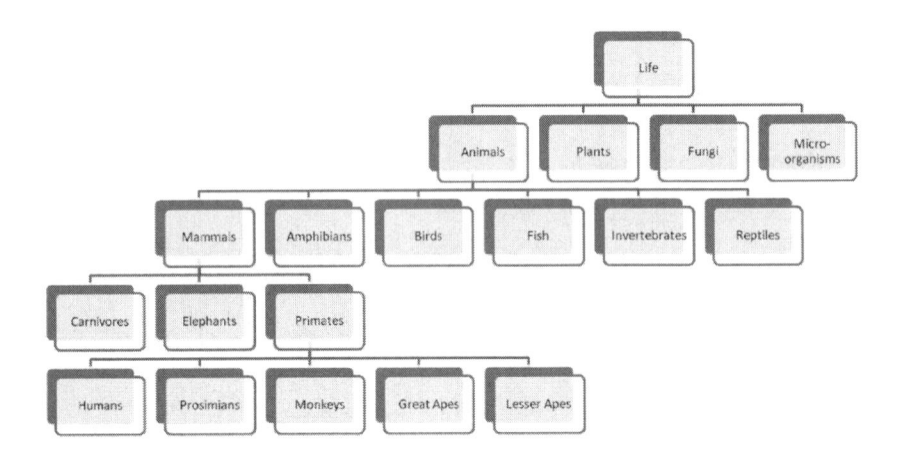

```
                                    Life
         ┌──────────┬──────────┬──────────┐
       Animals    Plants     Fungi    Micro-organisms
   ┌────┬────┬────┬────┬────┐
Mammals Amphibians Birds Fish Invertebrates Reptiles
   ┌────┬────┐
Carnivores Elephants Primates
   ┌────┬────┬────┬────┐
Humans Prosimians Monkeys Great Apes Lesser Apes
```

*How does Chunking Up and Chunking Down relate to the WHAT section in the SAS?*

Different people in the audience are likely to work at different levels in the hierarchy. Let's imagine we are presenting to the board or shareholders – they will most likely want big picture communications talking about the longer-term strategic vision. If you were talking to the manufacturing plant they are more likely to want to know about widgets per minute on line 1!

Of course, I'm generalising, but often the higher up the management tiers you go, the higher up the Hierarchy Of Ideas the conversations and presentations are likely to be.

'BUT', I hear you cry, *'my MD is always in the detail'*. The key reasons I've observed why this may be the case are:

1. If they have a preference for the **'Information'** personality type.

2. If their background is in the detail e.g. engineering, finance, IT.

3. They may be concerned about a specific thing/problem.

Generally, once a concern pops up in an area, many managers' approach (rightly or not) is to dive into the details themselves, especially if there has been a problem in an area previously or it is a high-profile project.

**Low Performance Presentation warning!**

Avoid copying other people because most presentations only consist of the 'WHAT'. They only tell people what they need to know (not why they want to know it or how to use it).

*Three common WHAT mistakes*

There are three common mistakes made in the WHAT section – let me take you through these one by one:

*WHAT Mistake #1 – Not starting from the beginning, instead starting in the middle*

Typical presenters think the presentation is about them sharing their knowledge with the audience, rather than helping the audience to achieve their needs. They'll split that into the three WHAT chunks. For example, let's say they are selling a diet product – they might structure the WHAT chunks like this:

1. The product is portable.
2. It contains natural ingredients.
3. And you can try it with minimal risk.

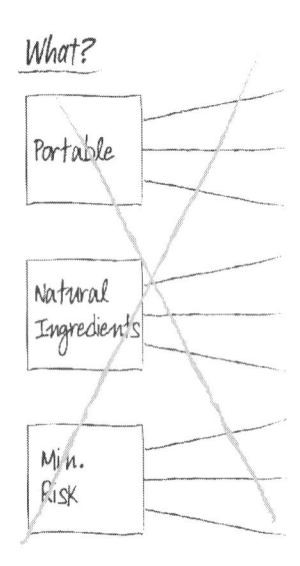

*What?*

[Portable]

[Natural Ingredients]

[Min. Risk]

This is fairly typical, a mistake made by all personality style preferences. It is based on what *you* want to say, what *you* have done and *your* world. But as you know by now, the presentation isn't all about you!

The problem with this approach is that unless I just happen to be in the market for a diet product right now, this won't appeal to me. You haven't sparked off a 'need' in me. I don't know that I need or want a diet product yet. You need to demonstrate first that I have a problem, and only then tell me how you can solve my problem.

In our diet product example, a better WHAT would be:

WHAT 1: The problem ...

  a) Are you overweight and worried about your heath?
  b) Do you lack confidence because of the excess weight?
  c) Do you find that no diet fits with your busy lifestyle?

WHAT 2: The solution...

  a) This new diet product is unlike others: it comes in packs of 7 sachets, so you can easily take one a day to work or wherever you go.
  b) It is made from Aloe Vera, so unlike other diet products that contain artificial ingredients, you know this has 100% natural ingredients.
  c) It comes with a money back guarantee, so that you can try it for a week and see that it works for you.

WHAT 3: Julie's case study

a) Julie was delighted she found it so easy to stick to the plan because it fitted into her busy lifestyle so well.
b) After just X weeks of using this product Julie was 10kg lighter and felt so healthy.
c) She's now super confident and wore a bikini on her summer holidays for the first time in 20 years.

The template would look like this:

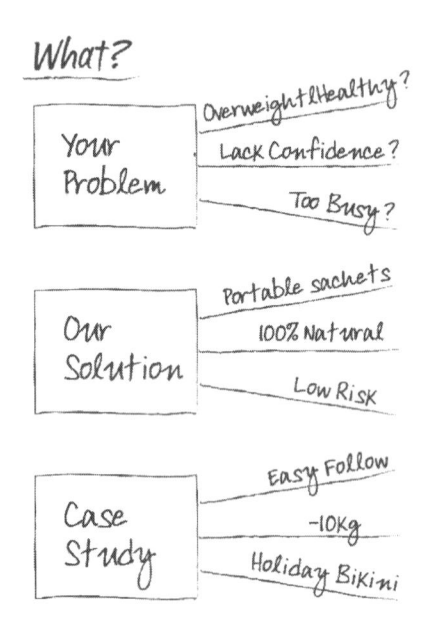

*What?*

| Your Problem | — Overweight & Healthy? |
|---|---|
|  | — Lack Confidence? |
|  | — Too Busy? |

| Our Solution | — Portable sachets |
|---|---|
|  | — 100% Natural |
|  | — Low Risk |

| Case Study | — Easy Follow |
|---|---|
|  | — -10kg |
|  | — Holiday Bikini |

Moving away from the diet product case study, then what could a business presentation look like? At a board presentation the keen professional will often dive right in and talk about their project status, or about the new product or service. Instead of doing that, this would be better …

WHAT 1: Background

You could show the 3 reasons why the project was established, what 3 key needs or problems it was set up to address or 3 key issues or successes in the last month/quarter/year.

WHAT 2: Current status

You might discuss your top 3 recommendations, 3 key actions you are taking, or the top 3 current results/research findings.

WHAT 3: Future

You might share 3 risks or opportunities we need to look out for, 3 predictions you have for the future or forecasts, or industry examples or product case studies you have divided up into 3 stages.

*WHAT Mistake #2 – Focussing only on features not benefits*

Another common mistake made by all Presenter Personality Styles. Features are facts about products or services – they add credibility and substance to your idea or sales pitch. Benefits give the audience a reason to buy into an idea because they explain how your strategy, product or service improves their lives. Benefits explain 'what's in it for them'. Persuasive presentations require a mix of features and benefits.

Going back to the diet product as our example, the WHAT 2 with features and no benefits would look a little like this:

a) This new diet product comes in packs of 7 sachets.
b) It is made from Aloe Vera.
c) It comes with a money back guarantee.

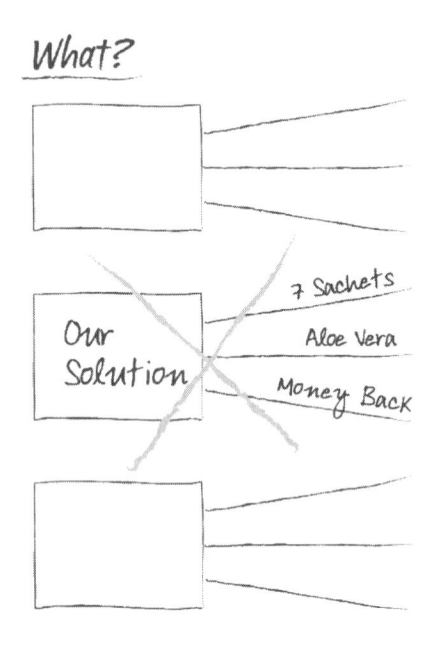

*What?*

[diagram: boxes connected to "Our Solution" with branches labeled "7 Sachets", "Aloe Vera", "Money Back", crossed out with an X]

Avoid this trap! Instead imagine you are an audience member and 'chunk up' by asking yourself a question like:

   a) 'What is 7 sachets an example of?'
   b) 'What benefit is Aloe Vera a part of?'
   c) 'So what? What benefit is the guarantee to me?'

Your new WHAT 2 Our Solution might be:

   a) This new diet product is convenient and portable – it comes in packs of 7 sachets, so you can easily take one a day to work or wherever you go.
   b) It is natural – made from Aloe Vera unlike other diet products that contain artificial ingredients.
   c) Low risk – it comes with a money back guarantee, so

you can try it for a week and see that it works for you.

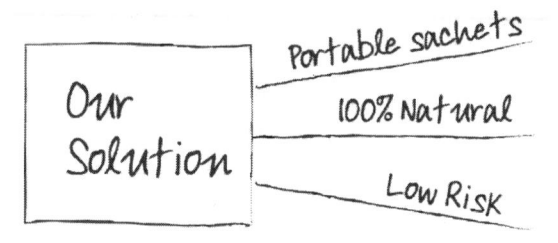

```
┌─────────────┐  ─── Portable sachets
│    Our      │
│  Solution   │  ─── 100% Natural
│             │
└─────────────┘  ─── Low Risk
```

In a business presentation context, typical mistakes may be:

- ✓ Saying the new machine runs at 2000 widgets per minute, but not that we can produce X more widgets because of that or reduce staffing levels by Y.

- ✓ Telling us the new product has the latest 'blah blah' technology but not that the technology allows the consumer to use it hands free, so we can drink our coffee at the same time.

- ✓ Asking for approval to buy new software accredited and approved by ABC body, but not that this means we can have peace of mind knowing that our data is safe and held securely to the highest standards, meaning our level of risk and insurance costs will go down.

*WHAT Mistake #3 – Understanding the potential*

As people often think about their product/service, rather than the audience, that also means they tend to miss off or undersell the results, often in WHAT 3.

This is a common mistake all Presenter Personality Styles can make. You may have heard of the saying that *'people don't want to buy a drill, they want to buy a hole in the wall'*. But actually, that phrase should go a step further. People don't want a hole in the wall either, they want the end result – the shelves to increase storage or a mirror to see themselves in.

In our diet study that translates like this:

   a) Julie was on the diet for X months.
   b) After just Y weeks she lost 10kg.
   c) It fitted in with her lifestyle.

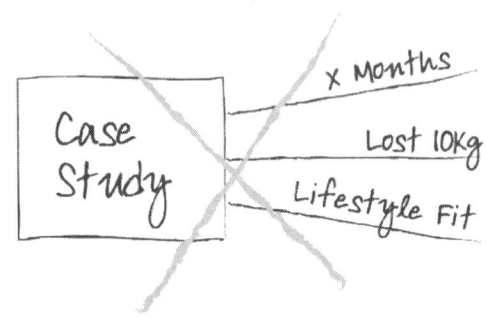

*(handwritten diagram: "Case Study" crossed out, replaced with "X Months, Lost 10kg, Lifestyle Fit")*

What makes it even better and stronger is making the results more emotional, meaningful and evidence based. Show how your product/service will benefit the audience into the future.

   a) Julie was delighted; she found it so easy to stick to diet X because it fitted into her busy lifestyle so well.
   b) After just Y weeks of using this product Julie was 10kg lighter and felt so healthy.
   c) She's now super confident and wore a bikini on her summer holidays for the first time in 20 years.

```
┌─────────┐─── Easy Follow
│  Case   │
│  Study  │─── -10Kg
│         │
└─────────┘─── Holiday Bikini
```

In the business presentation example, this may mean you haven't painted a vision of:

- ✓ The increased customer loyalty projection.
- ✓ The sales growth predicted in 3 years' time.
- ✓ The delighted team members and the subsequent reduction in staff turnover.

Final thoughts on the WHAT section:

1. When presenting, make sure you do your audience prep (**All styles**).
2. Make sure you know who you are talking to, and always do your best to address the topic at the appropriate level (**All styles**).
3. If you are more junior than your audience, prepare for the bigger picture approach (**Information** and **Caring**).
4. Always be ready for bigger picture questions from the senior team, for example *'How does this fit into our overall HR / Marketing / PR / Production / cost-saving strategy?'* (**Information** and **Caring**).
5. Consider the preferred style of the personality types in the audience. If they are likely to be more detailed, then be ready for the specifics. Have a few hidden slides, reports or additional reading ready to back up

your message (**Results** and **Sociable**).
6. If you don't know what to expect, make sure you talk to your boss or a mentor about how to approach the presentation (**All styles**).
7. Consider what the audience already knows and the range of knowledge or experience in the room (**All styles**)
8. 'Pacing' is covered later in Chapter 9. For now, you'll want to consider:
    a) How you'll pitch information that's new to some people and well known by others.
    b) The audience's current knowledge and position along the 'journey' e.g. Is this the first time they have heard this idea or are they very used to it?
    c) What external factors might impact on the audience that you might need to empathise with e.g. travel stress, time zones, personal challenges, financial results etc.

Pacing is relevant to all styles, though it's likely that those with a more extraverted preference (**Results** and **Sociable**) will want to focus on slowing down, and those with a more introverted preference (**Caring** and **Information**) may need to speed up.

It's not easy to comment or feedback on your specific content unless you are working one-to-one with a coach, but bear in mind it is highly likely you are the expert in your area. You know your content and message otherwise you wouldn't be in the role you are in[1]. Keep your expert status in mind as you decide what to include in your talk. The challenge for most people is chunking the message in a manner that makes sense and flows well <u>for the audience</u>.

Later there is an exercise where you get to fill out your WHAT in your case study presentation. You'll want to include an appropriate amount of facts, evidence and information and ensure this is displayed visually. However, first we'll cover the HOW section – otherwise you may waste a huge amount of time (the reason for this will become clearer as you move on).

---

[1] Even if you're starting out in your role, you are likely to be more expert in at least one specific area than the audience, so make sure you find your area (e.g. if you are new then you come with the distinct advantage of a fresh pair of eyes).

## The HOW section

This section of the SAS is all about the audience's short-term HOW questions:

- ✓ *'How does it work for me in the day-to-day?'*
- ✓ *'How do you want me to take action?'*
- ✓ *'How do you want me to respond to the information you have shared in the WHAT?'*

This is all about usability; it's about demonstrating the talk's relevance to the audience in the here and now.

If there is a varied audience, for example, finance, marketing and sales, you need to ensure that each audience type has an action relevant for them – even if it is small. It may be that finance need to be aware of the changes, so next time they talk to sales they'll be able to better understand their situation.

I am not exaggerating when I say that almost every senior manager I work with has not fully thought through the actions they want the listeners to take. Again, I believe this is a learnt behaviour from school and further education.

### *Rules for amazing HOWs*

- ✓ HOWs show the audience how the WHAT you've just talked about works in their world/can be applied in their field/should be used in a practical way.
- ✓ The HOWs should be relatively detailed and directional. You need to be crystal clear what steps you want the audience to take after they have listened to your WHAT.
- ✓ You can have a minimum of three HOWs – this tends to

- ✓ ensure that sufficient detail has been given.
- ✓ You can have up to seven HOWs if required, or anywhere in between.
- ✓ You can do HOWs in the room with the audience and give HOWs to do after they leave the presentation. In an ideal world you'd do a mix of both.
- ✓ If you really want to encourage action, consider taking the first step with them. This reduces the fear factor and gets them on their way through an exercise, practice, case study or group task.
- ✓ Position your HOWs in a manner appropriate for the audience. For example, if you are asking for buy-in from the board you may say, *'Do you agree with the key points I've raised?'* If you are a motivational speaker at a high-energy conference you might ask everyone to say *'hey yer'* if they agree this is really easy to use!
- ✓ Include appropriate timescales.
- ✓ Have at least one HOW that is relevant for each audience 'sector' e.g. UK, France and Germany.
- ✓ An advanced tip is to take the HOW into the future, beyond what you may perceive as the end goal – for example if you want to sell an item, the final HOW should be after the sale. Perhaps this might be a follow up meeting or a webinar to discuss feedback.

Let's revisit our diet example – assuming this is a high-energy sales conference and I want you to buy the product, the HOW might look something like this:

Example HOW - Diet Product

1. Write 3 words that describe your body now.

2. Write 3 words you'd like to describe your future body.
3. Discuss this with a buddy near you.
4. Decide when to start using your free samples.
5. Call me when you choose to order.
6. Or, if you already know it's for you, order right now!
7. In a month I'll call you to hear how well you are doing.

On the template summarised into two words it could be :

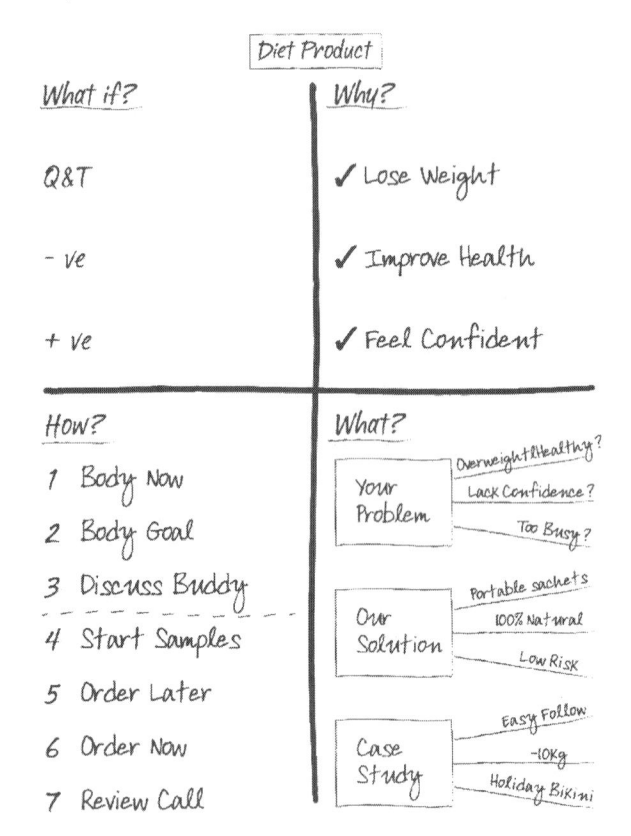

|  | Diet Product |
|---|---|
| **What if?** | **Why?** |
| Q&T | ✓ Lose Weight |
| - ve | ✓ Improve Health |
| + ve | ✓ Feel Confident |
| **How?** | **What?** |
| 1 Body Now | Your Problem — Overweight/Healthy? / Lack Confidence? / Too Busy? |
| 2 Body Goal |  |
| 3 Discuss Buddy | Our Solution — Portable sachets / 100% Natural / Low Risk |
| 4 Start Samples |  |
| 5 Order Later | Case Study — Easy Follow / -10kg / Holiday Bikini |
| 6 Order Now |  |
| 7 Review Call |  |

Moving away from the diet example, in a business presentation some different HOWs you might use are:

- Demonstrate the product/service live in the room.
- Show screen shots of a system working.
- Do an exercise or role play that enables the audience to experience the key points.
- Give the audience guidance or appropriately positioned instructions on how to use this thing, for example:
    - Use it ... in weekly reports.
    - Apply these learnings ... next time you sign in.
    - Pass on information ... to the customer.
    - Do it differently ... use a new process.
- Ask the audience to sign up to a newsletter.
- Ask the board to sign-off budget.
- Ask the customer to trial a new product.
- Ask the customer to place an order.
- Gain commitment from colleagues to attend a meeting.
- Gain buy-in from colleagues to a new idea.

## The HOW section and Personality Styles

### Sociable

You may not naturally plan the HOW section thoroughly enough. When you think through all the actions you may find there is preparation here that needs to be done way in advance (and if it wasn't for following this process you wouldn't have given it enough time) for example pre-reading, handouts or ordering samples or materials for exercises.

Your creativity will help you to come up with engaging ways in which to get the audience involved with the HOW section, and your flexibility will help you to adapt your plan appropriately on the day if needs be.

### Caring

Because of your preference for harmony you might be too indirect in your requests for action, resulting in fewer people taking action. Follow the rules for amazing HOWs, even though they won't all 'feel natural' to you in order to help the audience get what they need from your presentation.

Your empathy skills will help you to understand the audience and position your recommended actions in a friendly and non-demanding manner.

> ***Information***
>
> Because you like the facts, you may not always spend as much time considering how the audience should use the facts. People say knowledge is power, but it isn't. Knowledge is only power when it is applied (appropriately).
>
> Spend time considering the impact and effects of your knowledge on the immediate and wider teams, customers and suppliers. Clearly and appropriately guide the audience through their next steps.

> ***Results***
>
> This is often one of your strength areas because you like action. Your focus is to make sure your action steps include the people, on whom you are less focussed, and ensure you aren't too dictatorial (or the audience will feel it's your idea not theirs, and you won't gain buy-in). Avoid being too quick (or you'll lose buy-in) or too blunt (or the audience will switch off).

### *HOW section most common mistakes.*

- ✗ Not doing a HOW section at all, so no one knows what their actions are!

- ✗ Not pacing the audience – for example, asking for the sale at point 1, which is too soon, instead of gently pacing them and asking at point 7.

- ✗ Telling the audience what *your* HOWs are, not theirs! For example, at a board meeting this would look like:

- I'm going to crunch the numbers.
- Then I will develop the key ideas.
- Then I'll make a recommendation.

✗ Trying to achieve too much in one meeting – check the steps are realistic and well-paced so that you are asking for the next one or two steps, not the next ten steps.

✗ Telling the audience HOW the product/service works (that should be in the WHAT section i.e. WHAT do I need to know about the product or WHAT are the instructions for using it?)

✗ Telling the audience HOW the project plan works (that is WHAT are the project plan steps).

✗ Not being specific enough, for example, *'use this information'* – you need to be very specific and tell the audience how and where to use the information, for example, *'use this information towards the year end when you are processing the x y z'*.

✗ Not 'closing' the audience – you'll want to, for example, get commitment one by one, or confirm a date for work to be done by, e.g. *'Does everyone agree we need to have completed this by 31st March?'*

## Extra 'rules'

Now we come back to SAS bigger picture. There are three things or further 'rules' that require explaining, so that you can connect the dots in all scenarios.

1. What to do when the content is not chronological but 3

separate chunks of information.

2. A clarification of the order in which you deliver i.e. present the SAS.

3. Advice on the best order in which to prepare your SAS (which is different to the order in which you deliver it).

## 1. Separately – Creating a SAS with three separate chunks

On some occasions your SAS will more naturally fit a structure with three separate chunks rather than the chronological order we went through earlier. You probably won't know until you get going, and as I said, if one thing isn't working you can change it around. Let's assume you know your presentation WHAT is made of three separate chunks. Let's look at a new case study, for example, presenting at a company conference. The audience may need to know about company financials, a new product launch and a new software system that's being implemented. You could, in theory, do three separate SASs, one for each topic, but let's assume they are related in some way.

In this case you still have three branches coming off each topic, and you'll summarise them into two words as mentioned earlier. The key difference is that the HOW section is allocated into each of the three WHAT topics. So instead of the order of delivery being

WHY, WHAT, HOW, WHAT IF (we'll come to the WHAT IF section soon)

it now becomes

# HIGH PERFORMANCE PRESENTATIONS

WHY, WHAT 1, HOW 1, WHAT 2, HOW 2, WHAT 3, HOW 3, WHAT IF.

Your template would look a little like this:

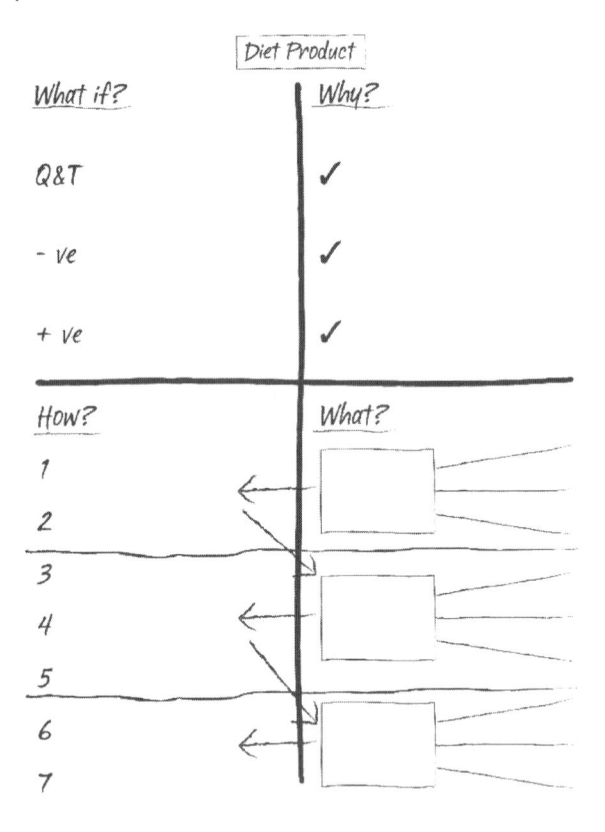

```
              Diet Product
    What if?         Why?

    Q&T              ✓

    - ve             ✓

    + ve             ✓
    ─────────────────────────
    How?             What?
    1
    2
    3
    4
    5
    6
    7
```

Using the company conference example and illustrative template below ...

# HIGH PERFORMANCE PRESENTATIONS

```
                    | Company Conference |
   What if?         |        Why?
                    |
   Q&T              |    ✓ Stay Motivated
                    |
   - ve             |    ✓ Save Money
                    |
   + ve             |    ✓ Save Time
   ─────────────────┼─────────────────────
   How?             |        What?
                    |                     ─ Last Year
   1 Tell Teams   ← |    Company          ─ This Year
                    |    Finances         ─ Forecast
   2 Report Progress╲|
                    |                     ─ Problem - Expensive
   3 Support Pilot  |    New              ─ Solution - Affordable
   4 Volunteer Next ←|   Product          ─ Evidence - Pilot
   5 Thoughts Share |
                    |                     ─ Problem - Slow
   6 Use Now      ← |    New              ─ Solution - Fast
                    |    Software         ─ Total Savings
   7 Working Group  |
```

You'll see that after the WHY section (which gives the benefits of the whole presentation) comes the WHAT 1 'company finances'. Decide what you want the 3 branches to be (note they may well be chronological in their structure). Then once you have spoken about the three branches you would move onto HOW 1 i.e. How is the audience going to use that information on company financials? The HOW 1 in this case has two points: 1) tell your teams about the excellent results and 2) report your progress at monthly meetings.

Then you'd move into the WHAT 2 'New Product'; talk about the three branches of how expensive the old product was, how affordable the new product is and the results from a pilot or test.

Next move into HOW 2 which has 3 points. Then the WHAT 3 with its branches, and then the HOW 3. Then you would move into the WHAT IF section.

Now you know how the SAS works for a presentation that has three separate chunks of information to be communicated (as opposed to a chronological WHAT).

## 2. The order for presentation delivery

To be clear then, when you deliver your presentation the order is always either

WHY, WHAT, HOW, WHAT IF

or

WHY, WHAT 1, HOW 1, WHAT 2, HOW 2, WHAT 3, HOW 3, WHAT IF.

## 3. Prepare your SAS in a different order

Above I've confirmed the two orders of presentation delivery.

Completely separate to that concept is the recommended order for preparing the SAS. We have worked with thousands of clients, and we used to do the preparation in the same order as the delivery. But as we're always looking for ways to improve, I read around the subject and then changed the approach, and clients have had even better results. We now recommend you prepare (not deliver) the presentation in a different order:

WHY, HOW, WHAT, WHAT IF.

This different order allows you to begin with the end in mind.

*How to prepare your SAS*

1. Do your WHY preparation first.
2. Then skip to the HOW section and imagine that you have delivered the WHAT – you've covered all of the information the audience needs.
3. Complete the HOW section thinking about what steps you want the audience to take.
4. Once you've done that, reverse back to looking at the WHAT section. Ask yourself WHAT information do I need to provide the audience with, in order for them to want to, or be able to, do the HOW?
5. Then complete the WHAT IF section, which is explained in more detail in the next section.

This process makes you, as the presenter, think about what the purpose of the presentation is and what you want the audience to take away with them. If it's not easy for you to get into the audience's shoes, doing this order every time helps.

Now it's time to work through the HOW and WHAT of your own example case study presentation.

## HOW and WHAT exercises on your case study

### HOW structure exercise

1. Imagine you're in the audience; answer the question *'What do I do with this information now?'*
    a. Write down the actions.
    b. Ensure min 3 and max 7.
2. Decide the best way to position this.
3. Make sure you pace the audience (See Chapter 9) and decide which order will work best.
4. Summarise your HOWs into two key words to act as aide memoires.

### WHAT structure exercise

1. Imagine you're a typical audience member like Julie or Fred. Answer the question *'In order to be motivated and able to complete the HOWs above, what three chunks of information do I need to know from this presentation?'*
    a. Sketch out several versions until you land on one you think works well.
    b. Decide which order will work best.
    c. Summarise your chunks and branches into two keywords.
    d. Reflect on which method of organisation you chose – chronologically or separately. Double check the alternative method is not preferable.
    e. If you choose to organise separately, allocate your WHYs accordingly.
2. Review your answers. Ask yourself if they are too detailed and, if actually, the audience would prefer a bigger picture communication.
    a. Adjust your SAS accordingly.
    b. Consider if some communication would be

better shared before the presentation e.g. holding a pre-meeting or issuing pre-reading.
3. Once you know your content, you need to make it engaging, especially these days as attention spans are decreasing. I cover plenty of techniques to help with that in later sections on interaction and engagement. For now, make a note to revisit this.

Your exercises on WHAT IF will follow in the next section.

Now you know the secret of the SAS, you'll no longer deliver or encourage others with unstructured presentations. You'll experience the magic of making your communications audience led, you'll find your presentations become more engaging and you'll see how you can apply this to your presentations (and all communications for you and your team) in the future.

Just get started and allow this process to be an iterative one that you revisit – trust me, it will save lots of time later.

Now you have your big picture structure of WHY, WHAT and HOW, let's say 80–90% right – it's time to look at the WHAT IF.

## End – The WHAT IF

The previous 'HOW' section was about more immediate short-term use, whereas the WHAT IF tends to address the longer term or bigger picture.

This section is about answering the audience's need for future relevance. It allows for clarification and consolidation of the message and further exploration of the content.

## The WHAT IF section

The audience at this point is asking:

- 'WHAT IF I want it sooner?'
- 'WHAT IF I want to use this in the USA?'
- 'WHAT IF I do or don't take your advice?'

The WHAT IF section is made up of three parts:

1. Questions and Thoughts.
2. Negative consequences of <u>not</u> doing the HOW.
3. Future benefits of doing the HOW.

This is where the Q&T (Questions and Thoughts) fit in because this is often an open section where the audience might ask, *'What if I do X – will it still work?'*

As you can see from the SAS template the 3 visual abbreviations are:

1. Q&T
2. -ve
3. +ve

We don't fill the template any more than with these visuals.

*What if?*

*Q&T*

*− ve*

*+ ve*

**Clarification questions should not be left until WHAT IF**

It is essential you check throughout your presentation that the audience understands the message. You don't want to wait until the WHAT IF for someone to say, *'I didn't understand slide 5'*. It is essential that people come along the journey with you and understand everything along the way.

There is pretty much no situation I can think of where you want anyone in the room to be left behind. If anyone is left behind it breaks rapport and you are likely to lose them for the rest of the talk. At best they'll become quiet and withdrawn, but at worst they'll distract others and that can be very dangerous! This is related to pacing the audience – moving at the right speed for them – which we'll discuss in Chapter 9. At the end of important sections throughout the SAS you might ask clarification questions.

Be really specific when you ask clarification questions and use a closed question, for example, *'Before I move on does everyone understand the key elements in topic 1?'* or, *'We'll have an open questions section at the end of this presentation and, for now, before I move on to talk about the new product, does anyone have any questions they need me to clarify around the company financials?'* (More on closed and open questions in Chapter 11.)

### WHAT IF Questions and Thoughts section

*'WHAT IF' are the only questions left*

Ideally, if you've followed this structure well, you'll have answered the other three types of questions (why, what and how), so you should be left with mostly 'What if?' questions at the end of a talk. Having said that, some members of the audience with a personality style preference for extraversion, **Results** and **Sociable**, may ask questions in order to cement their learnings. You might be able to recognise these because they come out a little bit more like a checking question e.g. *'So, you are saying ...'*

*Avoid asking, 'Do you have any questions?'!*

Did you know that by the ripe old age of 8 most people have learnt an automatic response to this question? Think about the last time you were at a presentation and got asked, *'Does anyone have any questions?'* What happens to most people is they automatically lower their heads and begin to avert their gaze to avoid any possible eye contact with the presenter. (It's those pesky Public Speaking Monkeys! Yes, your audience has them too!) They have most likely learnt this strategy in order to avoid getting picked on by a teacher at school.

Not everyone feels this way, but if you don't ever do this or feel that way then I'd suggest you are in the minority. So how can you do this differently? Asking questions is actually a bit of an art form, so I've created a list of top tips for asking the audience questions in a way in which they will engage and interact (see Chapter 11). But for now, I recommend you ask, *'What Questions and Thoughts do you have?'* This allows for those more vocal to give their thoughts, then others will begin to speak up as they feel more comfortable and see it is a safe environment. I often find it takes 2 or 3 people sharing their 'thoughts' before someone comes out with a question they actually wanted to ask.

*How to gain more buy-in*

In the WHAT IF section leading, closed questions can be useful. For example, after you have answered the audience's questions (or following on from an audience question) a closed question can be used to clarify levels of buy-in and commitment. Assuming you are pretty confident that you'll get a yes, you might ask, *'Do you feel the plan will work for your department?'* and then, *'Are you clear on the next steps you need to take?'*

### **WHAT IF Questions and Thoughts exercise**

1. Think about who is in the audience and imagine the typical audience member like Julie or Fred.

2. Write down all the Questions and Thoughts you might get asked – consider who might ask what type of question.

3. You can't possibly allow for the whole range of those 'What if?' questions, but there are always some more obvious ones you should prepare for, like, *'What if I want it cheaper, faster or utilising less resources?'*

4. Write down the answer to this question, *'What question do I really not want them to ask?'*

5. Next think of answers to the questions elicited above.

6. Knowing that creating your SAS is an iterative process, reflect back on your SAS and decide if you could or should include the answer to any of those questions in the original presentation. The changes could impact on any of the previous WHY, WHAT or HOW sections.

7. Amend your SAS accordingly. It is totally OK to leave some things in the WHAT IF section, but key points like timing or pricing might be better brought up earlier (or you may look as though you haven't considered this!)

## *WHAT IF wrap up section*

Finally, after eliciting their views and answering the questions, you summarise the whole talk in a short and sweet wrap-up. Yes, you do it AFTER the questions! Why? Because someone may have thrown a curve ball in the questions and taken you off track, or been negative about your ideas, and you want to finish on a high note and on topic. Here is a simple way to do that in just a few sentences.

Finish with a short answer to two hypothetical questions from the audience:

a)  *'What are the negative consequences of NOT doing what you're suggesting in the HOW section?'*

b)  *'What are the future benefits of doing what you're suggesting in the HOW section?'*

## *WHAT IF wrap up exercise*

1. Create a thought-provoking and motivating end to the talk:
    a. Think of 3 consequences to the audience of not doing the HOWs you've suggested.
    b. Repeat with 3 benefits.
2. Practise how you'll say these out loud briefly, so they flow.
3. Adjust your choices and language to ensure it is appropriate for the audience.
4. On the day, the wrap-up may change depending on the outcomes of the presentation so far. For example, if in the HOW you asked the audience to approve budget and if they have agreed to that, then you wouldn't want to mention in the WHAT IF, the negative consequences of not approving the budget (because they just did!)

Note: a version of this works in almost any speech!

Example WHAT IF wrap up
If you don't address all of these sections, in order, within your communications, you risk:

- ✗ Alienating the audience, because you are only talking about you and your products and services.

- ✗ Boring the audience, as they can't see or link the relevance or value to them of what you are saying.

- ✗ Losing the audience, as they can't follow your flow or story easily.

But when you do cover all sections of the SAS and prepare appropriately for your presentations and communications, you'll have more chance of:

- ✓ Hooking the audience in from the beginning.

- ✓ Motivating the audience into action.

- ✓ Overcoming any objections there and then.

# Chapter 8
# Final steps to completing the SAS, bringing it all together & audience interaction foundations

The final toolsets to complete the SAS are:

- Fine-tuning, practising and learning/remembering it to the level required depending on the context.
- Bringing the SAS all together and understanding how the sections all lead into one another.
- Learning about the audience interaction foundations to make your SAS even better.

## *The final steps to completing the SAS*

### Fine tuning the SAS

At this stage you have a broad SAS and now you fine-tune it by 'test driving' it, allocating the associated timings and then fleshing out the content.

Doing it this way may be a different order than you are used to, but it facilitates continual improvement and saves lots of time and energy later on.

### Test driving the SAS

The only way you'll know if your SAS is working well is to practise the presentation out loud and 'test drive' it – get a feel for whether it is on the right track or not.

Note: the presentation itself won't feel right at this point because you don't really know what you are saying, you haven't yet spent much time thinking about how you'll communicate your points. That comes later. For now, we just want to know that the SAS feels right and flows well.

## Test drive your SAS out loud exercise

1. Say your SAS out loud, top level, to see if you like it.
2. If your structure isn't flowing, then consider using the alternative structure layout.
3. If it still doesn't look or feel right from a structure point of view, tweak your SAS and repeat the practice.
4. When your SAS feels right, move on to the next step.

Now you have finished and are happy with the sections in the SAS, the next thing to look at is the timing. You do this before scoping out the content of your talk. **Information** and **Caring** styles might feel less easy doing this without the detail, but it works!

## SAS and timings

If you've been given a time limit then you need to make sure your SAS is appropriate to fit that, or ask for more or less time. It's considered very bad form to go over time as a speaker, so if you want to be considered a polite, effective and professional speaker, finish your talk on time or a few minutes early. It can be seen as bad manners to go over your allotted time, and you may be eating into the time of the next presenter. Even if you are the only presenter it's not really considerate to the audience if you run over – everyone has busy schedules and it's not easy for people to up and leave before a talk has finished, so try not to put anyone in the audience in that situation.

Shortly, in the next exercise, you'll see how to plan out your timings and before that I want to cover some top tips for staying on time on the day:

- ✓ Use a timer. For me, a simple watch isn't the best instrument for a couple of reasons: if throughout your presentation you keep checking your watch – so will the audience! Also you might look like you are in a hurry with somewhere better to be! I like kitchen timers (I never thought I'd find myself writing that sentence!) I buy small timers that are easy to rest on the table (they normally have a little stand) and click to start.
- ✓ Where appropriate, I take a full-sized clock: it's a light plastic one, so it can be stuck on a wall with blue tack. I pop it on the back wall and then I can check for time without having to look away from the audience.
- ✓ If it is a long talk, conference or training day, you could ask someone you trust in the audience to show you timing cards – make sure you know what you're doing and have practised.
- ✓ In formal conference arenas they may show timings on a TV screen facing you. But beware, often this is a countdown timer, so it can be off-putting and make you feel in a hurry! If you aren't experienced, ask them to turn it off and use the kitchen timer and ask for a '5 minute left' warning.
- ✓ Keep an eye on the time and look at the timings you have on your note cards. If you are ahead or behind schedule, there is no need to worry – just be aware of that and adjust accordingly; either catch up or slow down as you move forward through the talk. You may

even need to skip a part of the SAS. The beauty of the SAS is that it is relatively easy to adapt on the spot for last-minute changes.

✓ Be aware that you NEVER have time to spare until you are at the end of your presentation. It is more likely you'll be tight on time than you'll have plenty left.

✓ SAS is great for advance and last-minute preparation too. I went as a guest to a business event once where, because of snow, the speaker still hadn't turned up five minutes before the talk was due to begin. I grabbed the opportunity to speak in his place and used this structure to scribble out my plan on the back of an old receipt I had in my purse. I prepared my 'off the cuff' 20-minute presentation in just a few minutes.

✓ If you need to shorten your presentation last minute, using the SAS means you will be able to remain flexible and adapt appropriately. If you are on late or the last presenter – you may be expected to squeeze a 60-minute presentation into a 30-minute one. A good speaker does this without the audience even suspecting. You can do this either by covering only 1 of your 3 WHATs or by covering the same points in less depth.

## SAS timings exercise

1. Allocate timings to each section and branch of your SAS. Of course, you don't know exactly yet but you are likely to have some idea, so begin with a rough estimate.
2. Review both examples shown below:
    a. The 60-minute diet product presentation
    b. The 45-minute company conference case study
3. Allocate your timings to each of the sections and subsections of your case study presentation.

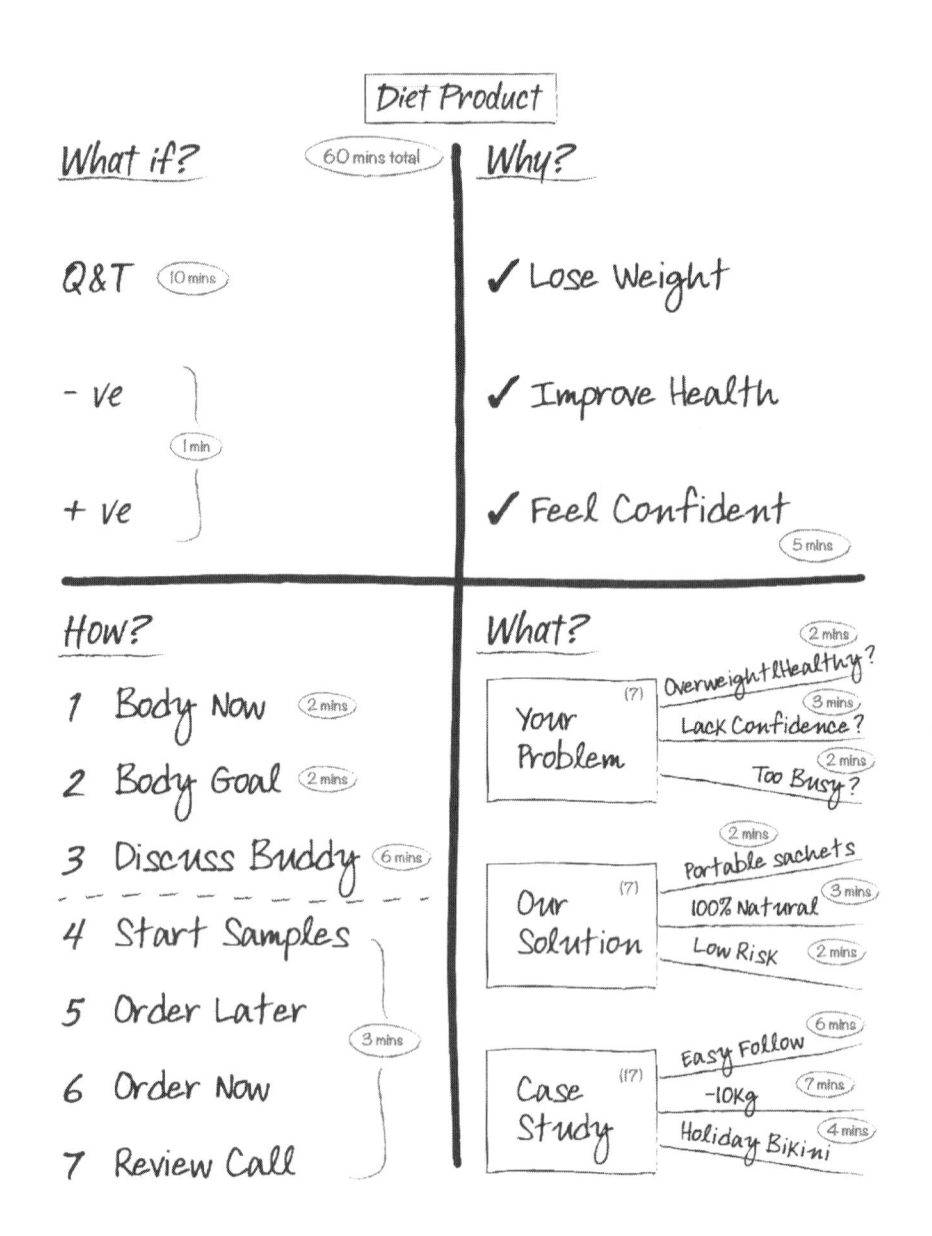

# HIGH PERFORMANCE PRESENTATIONS

**Diet Product** (60 mins total)

## What if?

Q&T (10 mins)

− ve  ⎫
         ⎬ (1 min)
+ ve  ⎭

## Why?

✓ Lose Weight

✓ Improve Health

✓ Feel Confident (5 mins)

## How?

1. Body Now (2 mins)
2. Body Goal (2 mins)
3. Discuss Buddy (6 mins)
- - - - - - - - - - - -
4. Start Samples ⎫
5. Order Later    ⎬ (3 mins)
6. Order Now     ⎭
7. Review Call

## What?

**Your Problem** (?) — Overweight/Healthy? (2 mins), Lack Confidence? (3 mins), Too Busy? (2 mins)

**Our Solution** (?) — Portable sachets (2 mins), 100% Natural (3 mins), Low Risk (2 mins)

**Case Study** (?) — Easy Follow (6 mins), −10kg (7 mins), Holiday Bikini (4 mins)

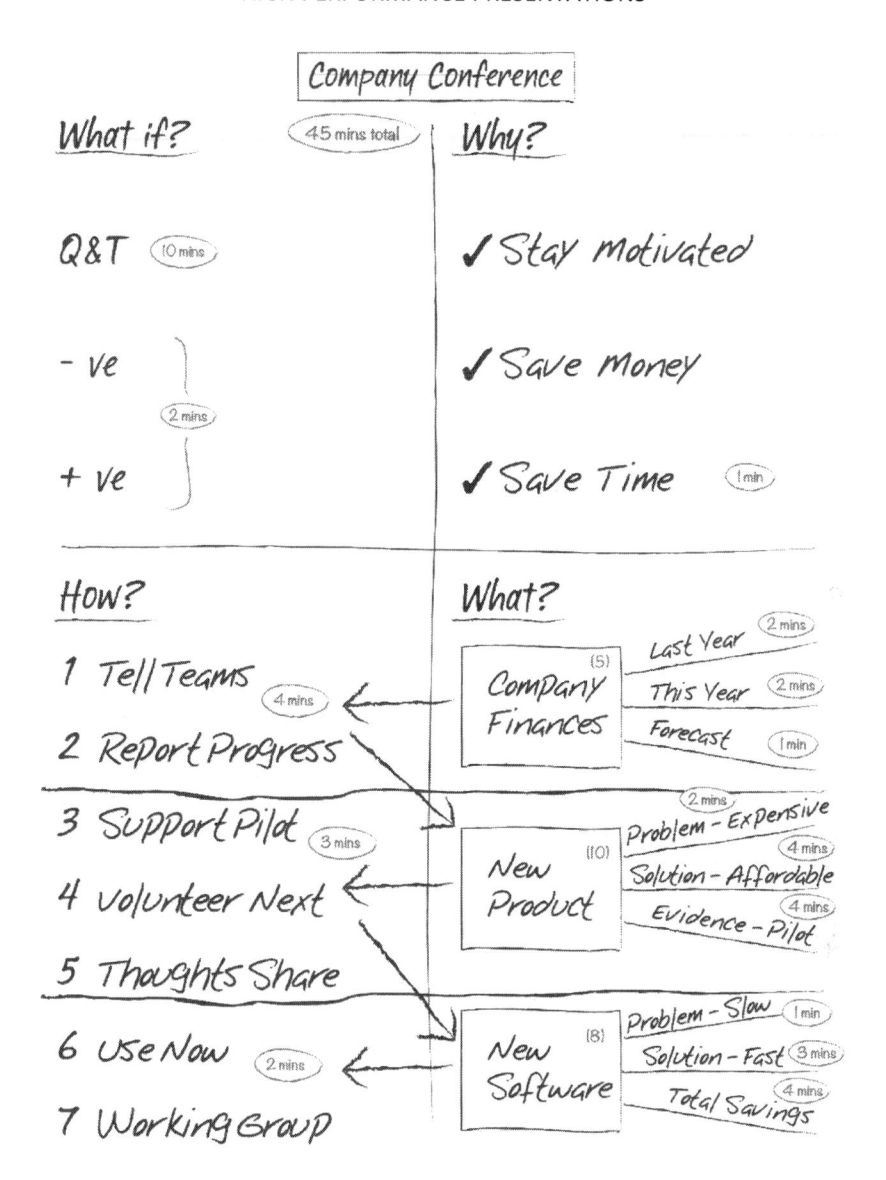

HIGH PERFORMANCE PRESENTATIONS

Company Conference
(45 mins total)

**What if?**

Q&T (10 mins)

− ve ⎫
        ⎬ (2 mins)
+ ve  ⎭

**Why?**

✓ Stay Motivated

✓ Save Money

✓ Save Time (1 min)

**How?**

1 Tell Teams (4 mins)
2 Report Progress
3 Support Pilot (3 mins)
4 Volunteer Next
5 Thoughts Share
6 Use Now (2 mins)
7 Working Group

**What?**

Company Finances (5) → Last Year (2 mins) / This Year (2 mins) / Forecast (1 min)

New Product (10) → Problem – Expensive (2 mins) / Solution – Affordable (4 mins) / Evidence – Pilot (4 mins)

New Software (8) → Problem – Slow (1 min) / Solution – Fast (3 mins) / Total Savings (4 mins)

## Finally you can flesh out your content!

Only now do you get to flesh out the content. Depending on the timings, you may only have a few minutes to talk about one branch. In the example shown, a 45-minute conference presentation might sound like a long time, but when we break it up into the appropriate sections actually no branch is longer than 4 minutes. At this stage people often realise they are trying to cover too much in one go. Do not progress! Change the SAS accordingly or get more time.

**Information** and **Caring** especially take note: if you'd spent lots of time scoping out the content, creating PowerPoint graphs and researching the topics before now, that time could have been wasted. **Sociable** take note: you'll need to keep your message clear and concise – too much 'off-piste' might take up valuable time.

## Flesh out your content exercise

1. Bearing in mind the timings, start to consider what content you'll include and what you'll leave out or put into the hidden slides if you are using PowerPoint.
2. Now you've allocated time to your SAS, you can relax knowing that each branch will last for X minutes or less.
3. With that in mind, decide what key things you need to talk about and flesh out the content appropriately.
4. This does not mean writing a script on paper or on PowerPoint! (If you don't know how to flesh out content without writing virtual scripts then read the next section on notes before proceeding with this exercise.)
5. For longer presentations, over an hour or so, the SAS is

still used. The difference is that you might drill down into more detail on a few branches. How many sub branches would you drill down into? That's right ... three! In the illustration below, WHAT 2, branch 1 has drilled down into 3 sub branches, as has WHAT 3, Branch 2.

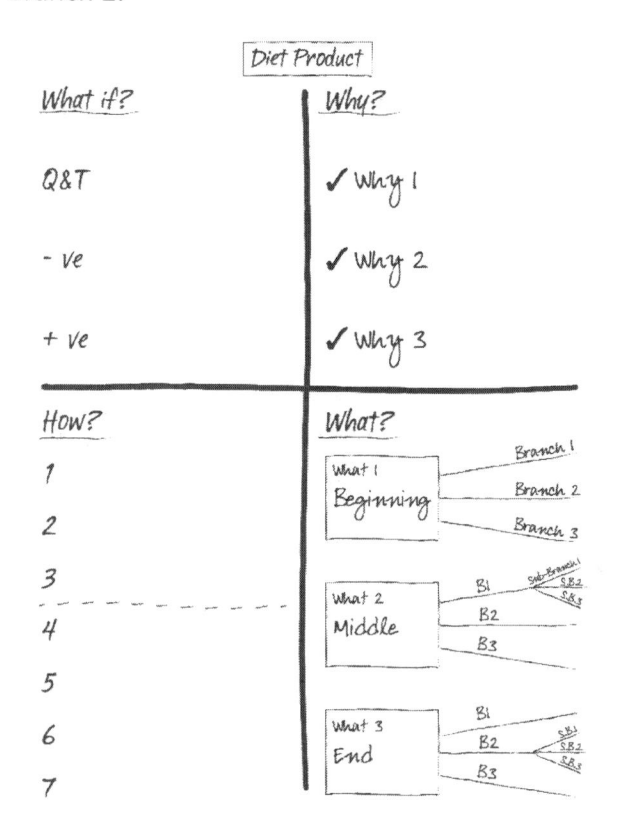

```
                       | Diet Product |
    What if?           |    Why?
                       |
       Q&T             |   ✓ Why 1
                       |
       - ve            |   ✓ Why 2
                       |
       + ve            |   ✓ Why 3
  _____|_____
                       |
       How?            |    What?
                       |                          Branch 1
        1              |   | What 1 |             Branch 2
                       |   | Beginning|           Branch 3
        2              |
                       |                     B1    Sub-Branch 1
        3              |                           SB 2
        - - - - - - -  |   | What 2 |       B2    SB 3
        4              |   | Middle |       B3
                       |
        5              |
                       |                     B1    SB 1
        6              |   | What 3 |       B2    SB 2
                       |   | End    |       B3    SB 3
        7              |
```

6. At this point in the process it would be good to consider what visual aids, metaphors or hand movements will help to succinctly convey the message. We'll talk more about that later in Chapter 10 and 11.

Once you have established your presentation content following the SAS, the next stage is to practise the SAS using aide memoires in the form of note cards.

## Practising SAS

Many of the clients we work with admit to previously not practising their presentations at all, unless it was a huge conference presentation, for example. Other clients admit to previously practising too much and trying to learn their script word for word. After we've worked with them they can see the benefits of practice and learning appropriately.

The most common objection is, *'I don't have time'*, but spending time on this section saves time later on.

- You'll make fewer last minute changes.
- The creation of your presentation slides will be quicker.
- Others around you will be clearer on the message so there will be fewer mistakes in implementation.

We know real life is pressured and other things are on your agenda, so we've developed a time-efficient way for you to practise even if you only have 5 minutes (though we hope you have more than that to spend on an important message!)

> We strongly recommend practising first, then learning the key points of the presentation – which seems counterintuitive.

### Note cards as an aide memoire

We always recommend using record/index cards to help annotate the key points instead of scripts or notes within

PowerPoint. This is the technique I've used with hundreds of clients and it works for pretty much everyone. The benefit of the method I'm just about to share is that it allows your personality to come into play, rather than you clinging to a script or PowerPoint slides. Your talk will be conversational and friendly in style, yet structured and professional too.

Depending on what type of presentation you are giving, having a few notes to refer to is often acceptable. If not, use this same technique I'm going to show you shortly, then just learn it well enough to not need the notes on the day.

But for some of you I can hear an objection – '*I need my notes*' or '*I need my slides*'! Let me spend some time sharing with you why that might be the cause of many issues ...

> **Being glued to your notes or PowerPoint slides activates the Downward Spiral leading to unnatural, boring, lifeless presentations**

Being tied to the lectern reading or relying too much on notes when presenting is often a sign of a lack of confidence – though it may not be obvious as these people can come across as 'OK presenters' if they are well-practised. The problem is that their personality and credibility can't shine through because they are so concerned about getting the right words out and not making a mistake. Senior Management are often looking to improve their 'open and trusted' scores on employee surveys. Perhaps they should look to their own speaking persona – is it natural or artificial? This ties back in with congruency and trust.

The Downward Spiral causes unnatural, boring, lifeless presentations. Let me explain how this works. Let's say the presenter writes every word down that they want to say on a script. Then they will read from it, hide behind it and desperately try to get every word right. But unless you are trained well – like Barack Obama or a newsreader – it is very likely you won't do it well.

Those with PowerPoint crutches want to read everything from their slides, so can't make eye contact with the audience and often end up turning their backs to the audience.

*My notes are paraphrased on this slide*

Either way, they are so keen to get the words right that they don't effectively communicate the meaning of the message.

Ironically, by having every word written down you are more likely to get your words wrong! You are no longer following the meaning in your mind, you have disengaged that part of the brain that forms sentences (something you do easily everyday) and are handing responsibility over to the 'reading-out-loud' part of the brain. That part of your brain may not have been used much since school days, and those memories might not be great, putting you into a worse state!

Let's say you make a small error when reading out loud, reading 'master' instead of 'muster', or 'chef 'instead of 'chief'. You then bury your head further, putting you into a worse state again! Your head is now down, you don't project your voice, make no eye contact; you then can't see how the audience are reacting, so you have no idea if they love it or hate it and can't adapt accordingly.

Then perhaps you start to speed up to get it over and done

with and things just get worse. The few people who were following now can't understand you and begin to drift off with everyone else. The round of applause at the end signifies relief that you've finished!

Even if you get every word right, the result is almost never as good as a presenter who is communicating 'live' because even if they get the actual words wrong, they still communicate their emotions and passion more effectively – and it is emotion that influences and sells.

Of course, the idea of getting words wrong may terrify some people and, if that's you, watch out – I'd say that's a little Public Speaking Monkey warning!

Public Speaking Monkeys can happen irrespective of Presenter Personality Style preference, and sometimes exaggerate preference traits. 'Tame' any monkeys, and then use the SAS structure and the note card technique and you will avoid this Downward Spiral.

**Warning – are you or the boss feeding the monkeys?**

If you have a boss (or are the boss) who likes to be in control or needs to cover every detail (often a **Results** or **Information** preference), they may be feeding other people's Script Monkeys! If the boss keeps telling presenters what exact things to say they will be writing it down and thinking they have to say those words. If you follow the SAS approach then the buy-in stage should happen now at this stage, weeks or months in advance. Not days or hours before going on stage. If that's you feeding the monkeys, stop it! If it's your boss buy them this book! Seriously take charge of getting buy-in and approval early, talk them through the SAS in advance and ask them to support your new approach.

## Writing your note cards exercise

These simple techniques work well across all learning styles. (Whether you end up ultimately using the note cards on the day or not is irrelevant because the note card step is important anyway to remember your key points.) Take note if you normally over-prepare (**Information** and **Caring**) or under-prepare (**Results** and **Sociable**).

1. Review the example note cards shown for the company conference case study below.
2. For your case study presentation write a note card for each of the WHY, WHAT, HOW and WHAT IF sections. If there are three WHATs and two HOWs, that will be three and two cards, respectively.
3. Write no more than 3 key points on each index card, no more than 2 words per point (transcribe the two key words from the SAS onto the card).
4. Accompany each key point with a visual that reminds you of that point. This visual must be hand-drawn, simple and relevant.
5. Number each index card in case you drop them, so you can quickly reorder.

HIGH PERFORMANCE PRESENTATIONS

**Company Conference**

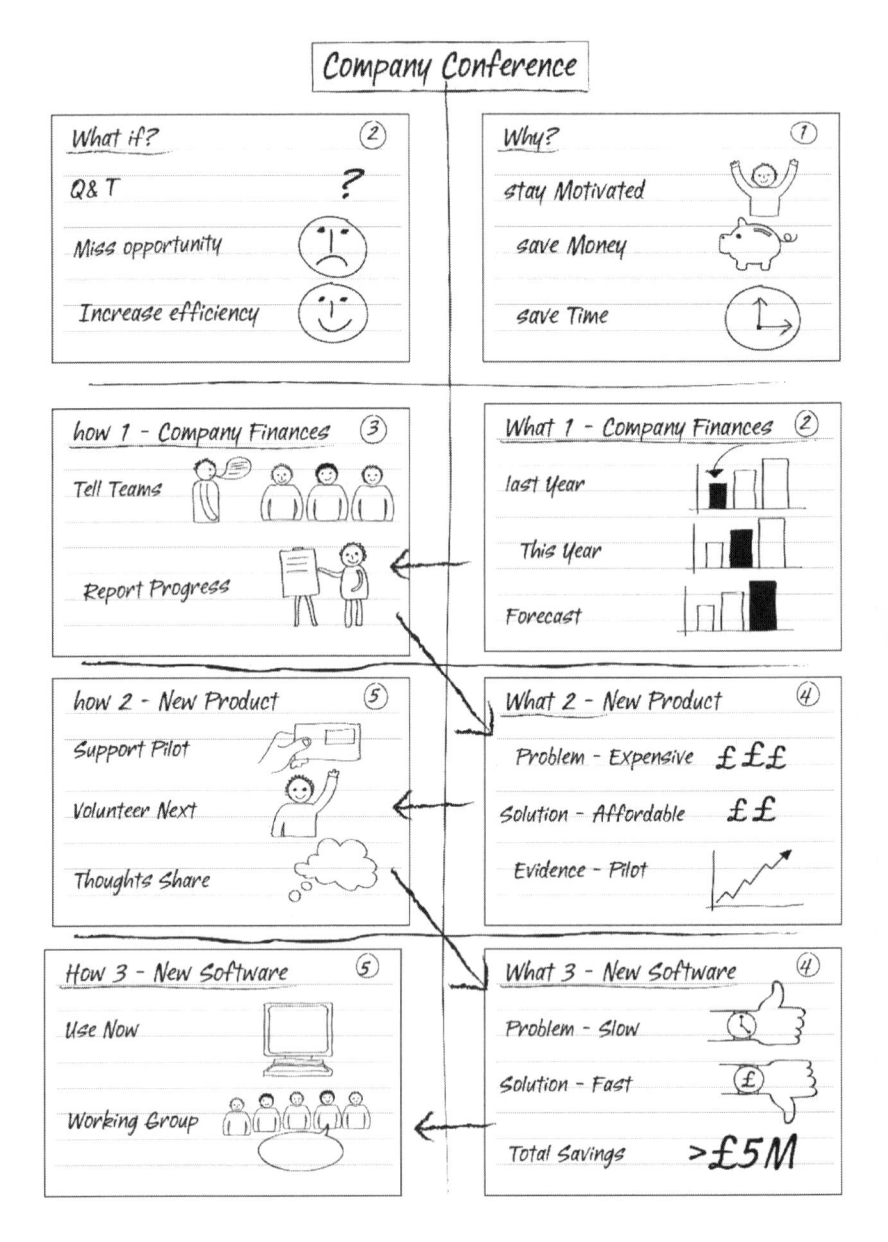

| What if? ② | Why? ① |
|---|---|
| Q & T  ? | Stay Motivated |
| Miss opportunity ☹ | Save Money 🐷 |
| Increase efficiency ☺ | Save Time 🕐 |

| how 1 – Company Finances ③ | What 1 – Company Finances ② |
|---|---|
| Tell Teams 👥👥👥 | Last Year ▁▃▆ |
| Report Progress 📋 | This Year ▁▅▃ |
|  | Forecast ▁▃▂ |

| how 2 – New Product ⑤ | What 2 – New Product ④ |
|---|---|
| Support Pilot ✋💳 | Problem – Expensive £££ |
| Volunteer Next 🙋 | Solution – Affordable ££ |
| Thoughts Share 💭 | Evidence – Pilot 📈 |

| How 3 – New Software ⑤ | What 3 – New Software ④ |
|---|---|
| Use Now 🖥 | Problem – Slow 👍 |
| Working Group 👥👥👥 | Solution – Fast 👎 |
|  | Total Savings  >£5M |

6. Learn each card individually using the Visual Memory strategy as follows:

   a. Think back to the colour of your first car or the colour of the room you grew up in.

172

     b. Notice the direction in which your eyes look i.e. do they look up to your right or up to your left? Perhaps sideways to the right or left, or down to the right or left.
     c. The majority of people's eyes go up and to the left and it doesn't matter, wherever yours go is just fine! This tells you where you go to remember visuals.
     d. One at a time, put each card in the direction where your eyes look to remember visuals and 'see' the note card. See it like a picture (rather than 'read' it out loud for example – you aren't trying to learn this parrot fashion).
7. Test yourself with the cards or ask a buddy to help you.
8. As you begin to get the hang of it, ask your buddy to test you randomly and out of order, for example ask, *'On the WHAT 2 card, what is the third picture?'*
9. In addition to remembering the cards individually, get to know where each card fits within the SAS.

## Practise your SAS with note cards exercise

1. Place all the cards on the table face up in an imaginary SAS grid.
2. Depending on how easily you learnt the cards, do your first practise with the cards face up. Run through your SAS out loud as if you were presenting for real.
3. As you get more confident, turn the cards face down and practise without seeing them. Peek if you need to.
4. Trust you know your speech, with a little help from the cards to keep you on track.
5. If you get a little stuck on one or two elements on the

cards just practise those.
   a. Practise only the parts that you don't remember as easily as the rest – don't keep running through the entire presentation.
   b. Start your mini practice from the end of the section you do know. Run through the section you don't know as well and finish on the beginning of a section you do know.
   c. This aids flow by ensuring that all mini practices are within the correct place in the presentation, not treated as standalone pieces.
6. Once you have practised your presentation using the cards, pop them into an ordered pile and refer to them only when needed. You'll be amazed by how much you remember. The benefit of using this approach is that it allows your personality to come into play.
7. Getting your timing right is an important part of your practice. To help, write on each note card how long each section takes and how many cumulative minutes into the presentation you should be. Use a small kitchen timer and have it counting upwards. As you practise keep an eye on the timer and cumulative time. You should aim to stay mostly on track or adapt your proposed timings accordingly.
8. Practise saying it out loud. With a big audience, add in additional time for laughter (hopefully) or engagement exercises. Even rounding people up from a break can take a few minutes.
9. When you're actually presenting, leave the cards face down and to one side.
10. Keep a glass of water next to your cards. If you want to

re-gather your thoughts, or check your timings, slowly wander over to your water and take a sip. Keep your timer next to the glass and cards, so you can easily glance down and check where you are.

For really important presentations, where you can't use your notes, you'll need to put in a little more time to ensure your key points have been totally committed to memory by completing the exercise below. I really don't encourage you to commit anything to memory word for word (unless there is a very good reason). But to get more familiar with the key points and flow of your presentation in the easiest way, it's a good idea to think about what kind of learner you are and complete the next exercise.

## Learning and remembering your SAS exercise

1. If you learn best by hearing things or talking out loud, you can use voice recorder technology to listen to yourself when practising.
    a. As you listen back through your talk you can re-think anything that's not easy to say or add emotion or additional interesting points.
    b. Use a voice recorder to record your full presentation (on your phone for example).
    c. Listen to it several times – in the car, while walking, or even as you're going to sleep.
    d. Practise talking along with the recording (not word for word!)
    e. Pause it if you get stuck – the flow will either come to you or you can play it back.

2. If you're a visual learner, and have got rid of all your monkeys, you could try the same exercise but substitute the recording for a video of your presentation that you watch back.
3. Check your voice to see where you need to add more emphasis.
4. Review your posture (see Chapter 10) and reflect on where you might want to add more emotion or additional interest points.
5. You know you are on track with your practices when they are approximately the same time every time. As you practise, your talk should be different every time (because you aren't learning a script). You are doing well when you are consistently covering your key points and hitting the same timing, despite not using a script.

When people fail to use this note card technique, or aren't able to let go of their notes, they end up looking at their notes or slides instead of the audience; they remain rigid in what they say regardless of the situation and waste considerable time over-practising (or they feel they don't have time to practise).

When you begin to use this note card approach you will easily remember your key points and talk naturally around them; you'll be able to flex your presentation to the audience on the day (even if just small tweaks) and engage the audience fully.

## *Bringing it all together*

Some people might, at this point, understand the SAS but not find it easy to link the sections together. Let's look at that.

## Linking SAS sections

To give you a starting point, here are some ideas for links – make up your own too. (Don't learn these parrot fashion!)

### From the LITTLE INTRO into the WHY section:

- *'So, you might be wondering why you'd want to listen to this presentation today.'*

- *'Before we begin, let's remind ourselves why this CRM system is so important.'*

- *'Who here, like me, gets frustrated that we keep making mistakes, missing orders and upsetting customers? That's why I want to share with you this new process today ...'*

### WHAT section links

**For the WHAT sections:**

- *'I'd like to start by ...'*

- *'Let's begin by ...'*

- *'First of all, we'll ...'*

**When finishing a WHAT topic:**

- *'Well, I've told you about ...'*

- *'Those are the key points of ...'*

- *'We've looked at ...'*

*When starting a new WHAT topic:*

- 'Now we'll move on to …'

- 'Let me turn now to …'

- 'Next …'

## When moving into the HOW and WHAT IF sections

### When moving into the HOW section

- 'You may be wondering how all this impacts on your roles …'

- 'Let's consider how this affects you in more detail …'

- 'What does this mean for your department, how can you help?'

### When moving into the WHAT IF section

- 'Before I wrap up, what questions or thoughts do you have about anything I've said?'

- 'Prior to closing what questions or thoughts do you have about what we've covered today?'

- 'Before I finish off …'

### After the Questions and Thoughts:

- 'To wrap up … <u>if we don't</u> take on board this new process by January then we may continue to make errors, miss out follow up calls and potentially even lose customers … but <u>when we embrace this</u> change and launch on time we will be able to spot issues sooner, *increase our service levels and hit our targets.'*

- *'In finishing off then, if you don' t...'*
- *'So, to finalise ... if we choose not to ...'*

## Linking SAS sections exercise

1. Go through your case study SAS and consider what links you want to make between sections and subsections.
2. Practise your links several times.
3. Practise different ways to do the same links – this prevents you from accidently learning them by heart.

Now you know how to make your presentation flow easily, let's move onto the next point, important for anyone wanting to make their presentation more engaging and interactive, and ultimately effective.

## *Audience interaction foundations*

High Performance Presentations require interaction with the audience. Presenters need to be able to run successful audience activities, be able to answer questions easily and deal with any objections effectively. We will cover these three for now and some more advanced techniques in subsequent chapters.

## Running successful audience activities

When we present at conferences or away days, we find we are often the only one in a full day conference encouraging the audience to experience and use the information they've learnt there and then.

That's why I wonder if the most underutilised section of the SAS is the HOW section. This is where the audience applies your learning to themselves and their teams. They are visualising or actually using the information. To make the HOW section come to life can take a lot of preparation – but that's where the real change or 'light bulb' moments often happen.

Whether you are giving a conference presentation or an informal webinar you'll benefit from engaging your audience in a HOW. Here specifically, I want to cover getting large groups of people doing exercises because some presenters find it too daunting handing control over to 100 or 500 people in the audience, for fear that they will never get them back again! But in long meetings and conferences especially, it is essential that participants experience learning for themselves rather than just being 'talked at' all day long. It is all about usability and relevance and demonstrating the talk's relevance to the audience in the here and now.

Even if you don't do conference speaking read this section anyway, as later I'll ask you to reflect on your case study.

Let me give you examples of a few HOWs I've used when conference speaking.

I spoke at an Annual Conference, on Insights Discovery Personality Profiling, to 80 people for 90 minutes. My goals for the talk were:

- ✓ Help each participant understand their preferred style.
- ✓ Enable them to see what that means in terms of personal strengths and weaknesses.
- ✓ Facilitate their awareness of how to adapt their style to

interact successfully with others, especially those colleagues least like them.

I used a mix of card games, individual reflection and group work in the HOW section to help them experience this.

At another Conference I spoke to 200 women, for just 15 minutes so it needed a speedy HOW. I asked participants to discuss their actions with the person sitting next to them.

I would encourage you to do it every time, at conferences, on conference calls and in meetings, even if it's only for 1 minute!

## Audience activity exercise

1. Review your SAS and see where to add an appropriate audience activity that adds value to your presentation.
2. Consider your audience size and how many exercises you can do in the time available.
    a. Allow a little more time for organisation and instructions the more people you have.
    b. Decide what main feeling you want them to realise. The whole exercise should be set up around the feeling you want your audience to have, e.g. confidence, empowerment, etc.
3. When giving instructions to a large group of people, do it in very small chunks, e.g. say to your participants, *'Find a buddy, say hello and face the front of the room for the next instruction'*.
4. Consider what props you might need – does your audience need pen and paper, or are you putting something on the table or underneath their seats. Will they require access to flip charts, pens or stickers?
5. Adapt to the room layout.

      a. Consider seating – round tables create a different feeling to theatre style.
      b. Adapt your exercises if people cannot move around the room or get out of their seats.
      c. If the seating is in theatre style you can still do exercises, for example, you can ask audience members to turn to the person next to them and discuss something, such as '*Discuss your top 3 findings*' or '*Describe how you are going to implement this idea in your business.*'

6. Practise your exercise timings – it is very easy to let these breakouts run away from a time point of view.
      a. Always take a timer and be aware of the implications of overrunning.
      b. In working out your timings, remember you will need to allow time to do the exercise and (where relevant) to debrief.

7. Ensure your instructions are simple and easy to follow.
      a. Practise on a group of friends or unsuspecting colleagues (before the event).
      b. Ask them to follow your instructions (not second guess them) – to identify whether they work.
      c. Consider how you will get the attention back to you in a loud room. Have a buzzer or desk bell, or music that suggests it's time to regroup.

Now you know how to run an activity successfully let's look at another type of interaction – answering audience questions.

## Answering audience questions

One of the main problems with Question and Thoughts

sessions, if monkeys haven't been 'Tamed', is that the presenter's nerves frequently force an inappropriate response. This could be because a question has been misinterpreted, or because only keywords from the question have been heard, rather than the full content.

You may have a preference for one part of the SAS or another, and that's OK, but watch out for stronger feelings like worrying about the questions, getting defensive or appearing to others as oversensitive.

If any of the following things happen when you are thinking about, or actually answering, questions then you can't be 100% focussed (and may have a monkey to 'Tame'):

- Worrying about not being able to answer the question or giving the wrong answer.

- Thinking they are out to trick or test you.

- Nervous you'll not be able to find the right word in the right language.

Some presenters hate the 'formal' part of the presentation but are totally happy with the Questions and Thoughts session at the end of their presentation because they feel that they can be themselves. They would be happy to be asked questions all day long. These people often have monkeys around 'performing' the more formal side of the presentation; it's OK when they can relax and be themselves, but not OK for them when they have to do the official presentation. For example, they may have a *'You're Gonna Forget What To Say'* Monkey which doesn't show up when answering questions because they don't have to 'remember' what to say, they just know it.

Other people really don't like the Questions and Thoughts session at all. This can be the most feared part of the presentation because it is the unknown: they can't plan for it. Often when you drill down to the core issue, they worry they'll be asked a question they don't know the answer to. The fear of not knowing the answer then adds to the monkey fears. For example, their monkey in this instance may be around not wanting to look stupid, look silly or be wrong.

The extraverted preference in **Social** and **Results** might be quite happy answering questions on the spot, but introverted preference **Caring** and **Information** generally prefer more time to consider their answers. That's fine. That's a style preference not a monkey. And of course, the more you've prepared in advance the better.

The ideal mindset with which to approach questions is to be 100% focussed on the person asking the question, and the audience need.

## Answering questions effectively exercise

1. If you actively like the questions and dislike the formal part of the SAS, or if you actively dislike the questions and like the formal parts, re-read the Public Speaking Monkeys section.
2. Take some time to plan for the questions.
    a. Allow time for clarification questions at each stage as you go through the SAS (**Sociable** and **Results** presenters).
    b. Allow time for questions and thoughts at the end (this may mean you reducing the content).
    c. Plan, near the beginning of your presentation, to let your audience know you would like questions and when to ask them.
    d. Consider how in more introverted groups (**Caring** or **Information** preference audience) you'll encourage questions e.g. by giving them a

heads-up such as, '*I'm going to ask for questions in a moment. Please turn to the person next to you and discuss together any questions you have. Then I'll answer those questions.*'
   e. Have microphones and runners for larger audiences, so people can ask questions that everyone in the audience can hear.
   f. If you are not yet confident in answering questions plan a happy medium – ask people to write their questions on Post-It Notes as they think of them, and then ask someone to collate them. During an exercise or break, review the questions giving you time to reflect before answering.
3. Practise answering questions professionally.
   a. You can practise these tips around answering the question now – you don't need to wait for a presentation to do most of these – get practising in everyday conversations.
   b. Stay open, calm and relaxed. Don't appear defensive or abrupt with yes/no answers (**Results** and **Information**).
   c. Think about the question for a moment before responding (**Results** and **Sociable**). And before answering, ensure the whole audience has heard and understood the question, by outlining or repeating the question.
   d. Ask for clarification if you haven't understood a question. and check for direct confirmation by paraphrasing the question back to the questioner: '*You want me to explain …?*'

e. Keep your answer brief – don't make a second 'mini' presentation (**Results** and **Sociable**).
f. If it is a complex question (for example, about something technical) use a story or metaphor that helps the whole audience understand the question and answer.
g. Answer the question you have been asked, not the question you wish you'd been asked (unless you are a politician).
h. When you reply to a question, direct your answer to both the questioner and other members of the audience where appropriate.
i. Encourage everyone who asks an appropriate question with a smile or nod – reward the behaviour you want (**Information** and **Results**).
j. Remember questions are for the whole audience. Even though you are taking a question from one member of the audience, as a presenter you are still responsible for the interest and engagement of the other audience members.
k. Avoid answering questions that fall outside of the remit of your talk: *'I'm afraid that really falls outside of my objectives for today's presentation. Perhaps we can resume discussion of that particular point later?'*
l. 'Fess up' if you genuinely don't know something or find another 'get out' e.g.
    i. *'What do other people think?'*
    ii. *'I think it is about X%, but I can get back to you with the latest figure.'*

        iii. *'That's interesting why do you ask that?'*
- m. Once you have given your answer, ask, *'Does that answer your question?'* so you can give more detail if needed.
- n. Take questions offline if they are going on too long or are inappropriate.
- o. If you notice that audience questions take you off track or bring up topics too early perhaps:
  - i. Pay more attention to guiding the audience through your SAS.
  - ii. Tell the audience, in advance, what is coming next.
  - iii. Consider if you need to up the pace (for **Results** or **Sociable** preference audience members).

Now you know how to answer 'normal' questions effectively, let's wrap this up by looking at how to deal effectively with any objection that may come your way.

## How to deal effectively with any objection

When most people think of objections they think of them as arising after the presentation or talk. This is one type of objection. There are also those types of objections the audience have before you've even started talking. Most people don't pay enough attention to these. In fact, they deserve focus because they can prevent the audience (or part of the audience) from listening further.

The more audience preparation you've done in Chapter 6 the better. And of course, whilst preparing your SAS in the WHAT IF section, you will have noted down the questions the audience might have. Then you will have reviewed and improved your SAS (where appropriate) and been able to add in some objection-busting positioning, information or facts.

The mindset required to handle objections effectively is one of a joint resolution – to find a point of agreement and work from there. If you go big picture enough, you'll find you both want the same thing.

In order to overcome objections in the moment you need to do a little 'mind reading'. Sometimes if someone asks a closed question, a short response of *'yes'* or *'no'* may appear appropriate, or a little terse, so you may need to add a little more information, depending on the situation and Presenter Personality Style of the person asking the question. For example:

Q: *'Will we launch on time?'*

A: *'Yes'* (this may or may not be sufficient information for the person asking the question – they may have a deeper objection). And, in some situations, this could be seen as defensive – either because your answer has been too short or because there is a Mini Monkey causing you to become irritated that they even need to ask that question. You may be thinking to yourself, *'Of course it will be on time!'*

or you could answer:

A: *'Yes. I have double checked with production and they are confident we will launch on time.'*

This answer gives reassurance that the questioner may need in order to feel confident in your answer. Whilst you may not think it is necessary to give this additional information, if it helps the person asking the question overcome their potential objection, then it serves its purpose.

And, whilst the questioner might have the answer they need, the rest of the audience may be lost. You might add some context around the question before you answer. For example:

A: *'Yes we will be on time. We had issues with the last launch, but we have learnt from that and improved the process.'*

## Objections exercise

1. Review your SAS and consider what objections you might receive. Revisit your audience preparation, SAS and WHAT IF section specifically.
2. Consider how to overcome these.
3. Ask yourself, how can you prove or demonstrate that X is the best way forward e.g. with market research.
4. Demonstrate your credibility and head off potential objections with case studies or testimonials.
5. Consider where stories (of someone else having that concern, even in an unrelated field) can help e.g. if the

issue is persistence over failure.

6. On the day make sure you understand the objection fully before jumping in: is it money, time, belief etc?

We'll cover more on objections later, but for now if you only do this, you'll be way ahead of the curve!

## Wrap up

I know some people won't complete the final steps of the SAS, see how it all fits together or include audience interactions, but their presentations will suffer. When you include all these things you'll improve the quality of your presentation and be able to deliver HPPs every time meaning you'll position yourself, your team and your organisation for success.

Let's see how all these learnings so far have helped Rachel to begin to deliver High Performance Presentations in the next of our 'Success Stories'.

## *Success Story – Rachel Results*

Rachel was a very successful and driven 46-year-old Sales Director who could present to buyers until the cows came home, but when it came to giving internal presentations to the board, she hated it. No one could ever tell because she hid it so well. Her team, and even her boss used to say how well she presented, but she felt differently. She knew when she had to do even better. She'd not had feedback on her presentation style, but the boss did tell her she was too direct sometimes and she needed to 'bring people along', whatever that meant! Others didn't know she worked late into the night preparing for her presentations, so she knew what she wanted to say inside out, line by line. Rachel's Presenter Personality Style mix is **Results** preference followed by **Information, Sociable** with her least preferred style being **Caring**.

Rachel was one of three main contenders for the next role up, and although she wanted it in theory, she knew she couldn't apply because she'd have to do so many internal presentations and wouldn't be able to keep up the facade. She often felt that she was lucky to have got as far as she had … so maybe this was it … she had reached her limit?

Rachel didn't want to tell anyone at work about her challenge, so finally, after years of thinking about it, she knew she couldn't put it off anymore. If she wanted any chance of going for this promotion she'd have to deal with this once and for all. She got in touch and booked onto our programme, asking to start as soon as possible.

*We went through the process, starting with Monkey Taming, and together we uncovered a 'Not Good Enough' Monkey. After some digging around we found it originated from 8 years old and onwards, when she felt her parents always compared her to her older sister who was a 'straight A' student. After 'Challenging The Monkey' and changing her own unhelpful mindset she was surprised, delighted and ready to learn all the new skillsets and toolsets necessary to succeed. The areas from the programme that she said were game changers were:*

- *Learning the SAS structure and specifically the WHY section, which then impacted on the rest of the way she thought about the presentation. She really 'got it', that the presentation wasn't about her or her department, but about the audience and what they wanted.*

- *She loved the pacing in the HOW section – Rachel did confess to rarely giving a 'call to action' in her previous presentations (despite knowing all about them in relation to the sales process). Now she knew how to bring the audience along with her instead of either not saying what she wanted, or saying it in such a way (telling) that the audience just ignored it.*

- *Understanding how to let go of so much control, not learning the script parrot fashion, and being free to speak from a structure of key points instead. This saved literally hours and hours of practice time, meant no more late nights before an important presentation and improved her audience engagement levels.*

After the programme Rachel applied for the role and was successful. Looking back, she wondered what might have happened if she'd done the training all those years earlier? Still now at least she was where she wanted to be, a great job, a good work-life balance and her team heading for the highest quarter results in the region.

# Chapter 9
# Rapport – Working with the audience

Now we are moving into the skillsets section and I want to share a set of skills that have been proven to work and are frequently underutilised. Obviously, I can't cover everything in this one book, so I'm aiming to bring to your attention the skills that we've taught time and time again to professionals. When they learn these skills they realise they were either not aware of them at all, or they are aware of them (and even used them elsewhere within their life or work) but did not apply them as well as they could to deliver High Performance Presentations.

We will cover personal impact, presentation delivery and conveying information visually in Chapter 10 and being interactive, interesting and inspiring in Chapter 11, but before that the foundations need to be built and building rapport is the foundation skillset to presentation success.

## *Why is rapport so important?*

When rapport is broken the audience feels closed towards the presenter; they can't listen easily, and they will often feel trust is lost. Unfortunately, those people are likely to then express their views to others and any negative reputation is perpetuated. A Low Performance Presentation is one where rapport is lost or broken, and sometimes to such an extent that it is hard to ever gain it back from those people present.

A High Performance Presentation is one that builds and maintains rapport with the listeners throughout. Rapport is important in all communication, including presentations. Audiences who experience rapport with the speaker feel positive towards them, listen and are engaged. Over time, they begin to trust the speaker and ultimately are more open to being influenced by them.

## *What is rapport in the context of presenting?*

There are whole books on the subject of creating rapport with your body language, your tone and your words – and yes, all of that is very useful, in fact I often teach it, and I want to take it deeper than that. Rapport is all those things and more: it is about the feel of the whole talk or presentation. In order to establish rapport, you need to find common ground and be in some form of agreement.

> **People who are like each other, like each other.**

Note: Some presentations are designed to purposely break rapport with the audience, for example in a surprise or shock situation or in stand-up comedy. In this situation the presenter must be very aware of breaking rapport and have the skills to manage that situation appropriately – eventually regaining rapport.

In order to be fluent in rapport when presenting I've broken the topic into three sections:

1. Pacing and leading the audience.
2. Disagreeing and rapport.
3. Avoiding offending people in the audience!!

## Pacing and leading the audience

Pacing and leading are essential to inspiration. You may have heard good products described as being 'ahead of their time'. The same is true for ideas. If you present an idea ahead of the right time for the audience, they may not even hear it, or they'll dismiss it out of hand without properly listening.

You can ensure you build and maintain rapport with the audience by pacing them before you lead them, by which I mean, starting where they are before trying to move them to the new destination. It's about moving at the right speed for the audience.

Pacing is often a key objective in the SAS WHAT 1. To begin with, the strategy is to pace or 'mind read' by guessing what the audience are thinking right now and repeating that back to them. This makes them feel more comfortable, that they aren't the only ones going through the experience. They then become happier to join in and interact because they feel it is a safe, comfortable environment. This may not sound easy, but asking questions is a great way to begin.

Only once you have paced their current experiences can you lead and move on to present innovative ideas, alternative approaches or new news.

This may be best illustrated by an example I use: near the beginning of our presentation skills training we want to know where the audience is with their pre-prep. But to ask bluntly might not maintain rapport with those who haven't completed it. In order to overcome this, we might pace them by saying:

**Step 1 – to prepare and pace the audience I might say:**

*'Just so I can get a feel for where we are – who hasn't yet had a chance to do their pre-prep work?'* (Pacing their reality.)

Then put your hand up and wait for audience response.

**Step 2 – when you do this yourself you need to encourage people to engage and pop their hands up too.**

Nod at those who raised their hands, and to encourage further, whilst smiling and nodding say: *'Anyone else?'*

This is embarrassing to admit to, but by mentioning it earlier on, and with a fun approach, you can get an honest answer. After all, it's better to know than not.

You might want to reassure them (as now they are worried they might get left behind) and say, *'OK well, if there is anything that isn't totally clear as we go through, let me know'*.

**Step 3 – Then it's good to ask the opposite question to ensure everyone in the audience is involved, so I'd ask:**

*'And who here has done their pre-prep?'*

Then encourage those people to put their hands up.

And finally – you want to aim for almost 100% to have raised hands, so if not everyone has, you'll want to improvise to include the others – for example:

*'Who's not going to raise their hands whatever I say … or … who's here just for the free buffet?!'*

These types of questions are great at the beginning of the presentation, and also at the beginning of any new topics, to get a real feel for where the people in the audience are.

The point is that you've uncovered some sensitive information without breaking rapport, and you can now adapt your presentation delivery and level to match their needs.

Referring back to their answers throughout the presentation also works well; it demonstrates you listened to them too.

You can also use pacing to help you pitch your information at the right level. You might want to say, for example: *'How many people here are already using X product?'*, *'And how many people aren't aware of product X?'* and then, *'So the rest are aware of it, but just not using it now – right?'*

Once you have paced the audience enough, you have earned the opportunity to lead them. Leading is often a key objective in the SAS WHAT 2. This is where you need an awareness of others, often referred to as sensory acuity. Sensory acuity is the ability to use our senses e.g. see, hear, feel to make accurate observations about ourselves or other people, to see that you are leading them at the right speed. If you go too fast – literally or figuratively – slow down. So many great ideas are lost because the presenter didn't pace appropriately.

Mostly the mistake is trying to lead too soon. This breaks rapport and you need to start again – go back to the objective of pacing to regain rapport before you try to lead again.

The preferred Presenter Personality Style of the audience will be in play here. Those with an introverted preference generally prefer a slower pace of change and extraverted preference styles tend to favour a faster pace. Your audience is likely to contain both, so you have to be playing a balancing act as you go through.

## Pacing and leading exercise

1. Review your SAS and identify where you might be moving too quickly or too slowly for the audience.
2. Develop techniques to improve weaker areas.
3. Practise with a different personality style to you.

> Just so I can get a feel for where we are – who hasn't yet had a chance to do their pre-prep work?

Few presenters seem to notice that what the audience wants from a presentation can change over time. They fail to see that a presentation done at one stage of a project, or product's lifecycle, needs to be different at a later stage. You need to be clear, before you begin to even create your presentation, what the audience is looking for as the recipient (and what you are looking for as the presenter). Completing your audience preparation in Chapter 6 helps with this.

## Disagreeing and breaking rapport vs. disagreeing whilst maintaining rapport

Plenty of presenters disagree a bit too bluntly without realising the negative effect it can have on audience rapport. (**Results** preference may be prone to this by responding too quickly, and **Information** preference may do this because they are discussing the specific detail not the bigger picture concept.) That isn't to say you have to agree with everyone and be like a doormat either – but there are better ways to 'not agree' that do not break rapport.

This feeling of disagreement can happen in conversations such as the questions section of a presentation. If someone says, '*I think we should increase sales by 15% with this new product*', and you say, '*No, we won't*', then that is saying the opposite of what the other person has said. The problem with it is that it can break rapport immediately, and for 'breaks rapport' you can read 'breaks trust', 'breaks openness', 'breaks positive feelings' and so on.

In a typical work relationship where people are not consciously aware of rapport and how it can be broken with only one word, the other party may feel rejected or hurt. Blunt disagreement can come across as defensiveness and can be a sign of a Public Speaking Monkey. The words can come across as a lack of openness to feedback. But being open to feedback is critical if you want to get promoted or start that next role. For all these reasons it is important to learn how to 'not agree' whilst maintaining rapport.

Blunt disagreement can also happen when you are in the main part of the presentation, but it can be a bit trickier to spot if you are not in 'conversation' with the audience. That's one of the reasons why I suggest that you always aim to be in a conversation with the audience – to be interactive and always going back and forth (more about this in Chapter 11). If you have broken rapport, at least then you'll find out within a few minutes, rather than waiting until the end to find out everyone is in a huff!

If you are aware of the world around you, using Presenter Stance (discussed in Chapter 10) and Peripheral Vision to see what reaction you are getting (which I talk about in my first book), you'll know when you've broken rapport with an individual or with the audience – it feels as though they have switched off, disengaged, or become vacant.

Interestingly I notice professionals who 'argue' for a living can be guilty of this in their presentations. Litigators, for example, when speaking outside of the courtroom can break rapport (frequently!) without realising it, using the techniques they've learnt to 'win' in the courtroom.

Many people don't like disagreeing; they find it uncomfortable or stressful, particularly **Caring** and **Sociable**. The good news is that there are plenty of techniques you can use that still feel nice for both parties. Some people (**Results, Information**) actually enjoy a debate, and for those people it is good to find a communication technique that brings out the best in people with other styles as well – because they have a lot to bring to the debate, given half a chance.

> **You can disagree with someone without being disagreeable**

Whichever type you are, if you want to resolve an issue where perhaps you don't agree with someone, the best way to do that is to maintain rapport and work through it. You could use brute force or threatening behaviour – those with strong **Results** preference are sometimes accused of this – but these are not high on the list of managerial motivational techniques (and they tend not to work long term either).

The most influential way to maintain open communication lines is to maintain rapport and keep your ears and mind open! Aim for a win-win scenario, not a win-lose agenda. (Techniques covered in Chapters 5 & 12 will specifically help with this.)

## Potential disagreements exercise

1. Review your SAS and identify where you might have potential disagreements or objections.
2. Double check sensitive areas e.g. new concepts, innovative ideas and controversial topics.
3. Consider different styles and prepare your approach.

## Avoid offending people in the audience!!

There's a sure-fire way to break rapport and make a negative personal impact, and that's to offend the audience! Something might go down well with a particular audience, but the same thing in a different room might go down like a lead balloon. (Take note, especially **Sociable, Results** and **Information** styles.)

### Social no-nos

In my experience of training professionals, frankly some people are better than others at being socially aware – and the ones who aren't good at it are often not aware that they aren't! What I mean by social awareness is the ability to know and sense that what you are saying or doing is socially acceptable within that group.

If you've ever seen the TV programme, 'Fawlty Towers', you might recognise this line from Basil (played by John Cleese):

> **'Listen, don't mention the war! I mentioned it once, but I think I got away with it all right. [returns to the Germans] So! It's all forgotten now, and let's hear no more about it. So, that's two egg mayonnaise, a prawn Goebbels, a Hermann Goering, and four Colditz salads.'**

There are some obvious inappropriate topics you'll want to avoid – unless of course it is your job to talk about them. But assuming you aren't an international peace keeper, priest or prime minister then you might be best to avoid politics, religion, and death. You might also do well to steer clear of age, appearance, sex and personal wealth if it isn't relevant to your business.

Beware of generalisations made based on past experience or what other people have told us. The key is to be aware when we are doing it – for example, I often talk about the difference between men and women when they present. My intention is always do it in a sensitive way, saying something like, *'Of course I'm generalising and not all women do this, and not all men do that, but it helps to make a generalisation in this example'*.

It is also likely there will be some less obvious topics to steer clear of, depending on the specific group. There may be something in the company history that is inappropriate to talk about, such as a product recall or redundancies. It is your job to uncover whether there are any specific sensitivities, and either speak about them appropriately or not at all. If in doubt, check with someone in the know.

The skill of avoiding social no-nos tends to come with some personality preferences – if you are now worrying which you are and hoping that you've never accidently offended anyone, that may in itself suggest that you are sufficiently socially aware! If you are reading this thinking, *'Who cares, I just tell them straight, as it is, no nonsense – let's just get onto the next tip'* then it might well be that you need to take note!

## Avoiding social no-nos exercise

1. Be aware of your prejudices and avoid forming an opinion before knowing the facts.
2. Tread carefully around areas of prejudice like: gender, political opinion, social class, age, disability, religion, sexuality, race/ethnicity, language, nationality, and other personal characteristics.
3. When you have a big presentation run it past a **Caring** preference type and invite their opinion. (Don't do this last minute – give them some notice and make them feel safe in giving you feedback. Then they will be happy to help.)

## Inappropriate topics, jokes and remarks

Whilst researching for this book, people recited plenty of stories of when speakers told inappropriate jokes. The offenders in the stories seemed to more often be those in senior positions and over 50. Perhaps this is a coincidence, or because 20–30 years ago, when they were starting off the workplace, it was a very much less politically correct place. Another contributing factor may be that now they are senior, people don't feel comfortable telling them that their jokes are inappropriate, so as long as the HR director isn't in the room they are unlikely to find out until it goes horribly wrong! You may think the jokes are funny down the pub, but when told to a room full of a whole variety of people, the reaction will be quite different. Even if you have successfully told the joke to a room of 100s of people before, you may get a very different reaction from a different audience.

The disconnect can happen over almost anything, so my suggestion is to avoid telling jokes on any topics that could be considered sensitive in the first place. More and more we are becoming part of a multi-cultural business world, and even if there isn't someone in the room who could be offended, nowadays you need to remember that your joke could be tweeted across the globe, reaching other divisions, departments and customers.

It is not just jokes that can go wrong: there is the faux pas (the name given to an embarrassing or tactless remark in front of others).

When you look at how a faux pas actually happens, it is often the context that is the problem and perhaps the thing said would have been OK elsewhere.

**Avoiding inappropriateness exercise**

1. Using the audience preparation techniques will reduce the chances of a faux pas, but it is always worth doing extra research for all important meetings.
2. If you are going to a different country, check out the cultural dos and don'ts and body language no-nos!
3. Generally, it can build rapport to refer to something topical in a talk, so if you know what is going on, great – and probably best to avoid it if you don't.
4. Avoiding it doesn't mean being ignorant of it. Get all the information you can.

Side note: We mentioned the Autistic spectrum earlier, and

avoiding social gaffs can be challenging for those higher on the spectrum because they don't have the same understanding of context as others might. They might often say they were just 'telling the truth' e.g. *'she's fat'* and not be aware of the social norms around that subject. Or they may tell you that it was said in a previous context and it was OK, so why is it not OK in this context for example at home vs. at work. If you feel someone you manage or work alongside with may be higher on the spectrum, it might be worth doing a little reading around the subject to understand them better, and learn how best to adapt to help them have even more successful communications.

**Spelling, punctuation and grammar**

**Sociable, Caring** and **Results** styles take note.

I'm the first to admit that this is not my strong point, but since understanding more about the different Presenter Personality Styles, I have begun to appreciate how important it is to some people that spelling, punctuation and grammar are correct. Having said that, I also know from writing my first book that however many times a book is proofread it is still possible there are errors! Also, different people have different beliefs of how things should be written or expressed so it may not be possible to get it 100% right all the time. If you, like I used to, can't see the importance of grammar, punctuation and spelling then it is worth understanding why it is important to get it right – or at least minimise errors:

- Some people can be so distracted by spelling errors or inconsistencies that they then can't concentrate on the information being shared. Always avoid distractions in

your presentations.
- Some people will make a generalisation that if you can't spell correctly then nor can you do other detailed tasks correctly. Incorrect spelling or punctuation may lead to some members of the audience feeling they cannot trust your numbers or assertions, for example.
- It can hold back your progression. I remember speaking to the CEO of a very traditional British organisation who told me that they were very happy with a Director's performance except for one thing: when that person presented to the board, their grammar was poor. They felt this damaged the message and reflected poorly upon the person. You may or may not agree with this, but it was definitely having an impact on their career.

## Avoiding writing and speaking errors exercise

1. If you are unsure whether this is holding you back, ask for feedback from people in senior positions and/or **Information** style preference audience members.
2. If you know this isn't one of your strengths, then develop a strategy to improve. There are plenty of books and audios that can help you to develop your grammar, spelling and punctuation skills.
3. Ask others to proofread slides etc. Professionals are great, but even a fresh pair of eyes can help.
4. If you mess up – take it as feedback, learn from it and move on.

I like to write with a conversational style which may not always be grammatically correct. Running my own business, I have the advantage that if the potential clients don't like my style they can work with a Licensee with a different style or choose not to work with us. We want to attract clients who like our approach. If you want to communicate effectively either decide to mostly appeal to people who like your style or learn to adapt to the styles of stakeholders around you.

## *What next?*

Managing rapport is an important skill in presentations and in life. It's highly likely you're already good at rapport otherwise you wouldn't be so successful in your role, but if you don't apply those same skills to your presentations you risk missing the real objections, losing the audience or worse still, offending them! Now you can become really aware of maintaining rapport your audience are more likely to feel comfortable, open and gently persuaded at the right pace for them.

Let's move on to look at three more career-enhancing skillsets.

# Chapter 10
# Personal impact, presentation delivery and conveying information visually

You've probably been to a presentation that didn't work for you, right? And you've probably heard more than one speech that you wish you could have missed. If you're speaking but you aren't 100% sure of what you're saying, the audience is going to realise it. We won't go into depth on personal impact in this book – how to stand, use of voice and hands because there are tips and videos on my website to help you with that, (www.SimplyAmazingTraining.co.uk/body-language-presentation-skills/), but I would like to highlight the key areas that frequently arise in our training and mentoring programmes: personal impact, presentation delivery and conveying information visually including PowerPoint.

## *Personal impact*

Personal impact is about creating a strong positive impression on others, so they pay attention and listen when you speak.

Rightly or wrongly, human nature drives us to follow (and trust) high-impact or 'high-status' individuals, so if you want to influence and persuade, avoiding unconscious low-status behaviours is a good idea.

I like to use the example of a king and jester (joker). Imagine all the things the king would do and how that conveys high status.

Then compare that with what the jester is doing that makes him low status. The following tips will help increase your perceived status:

- High-status people allow their body and energy to expand into the space, whereas low-status individuals curl up – Presenter Stance (covered next) addresses this.
- High status is demonstrated by those who are genuinely calm and confident. Showing anxious energy will lower your status. It is often said that confidence (high status) isn't a thing in itself, it's simply the absence of insecurity. That's why it is so important to solve any confidence issues at their roots, rather than brush them under the carpet.
- Physical quirks and fidgeting indicate anxiety and discomfort, and emphasise low status. If you want to demonstrate high status, be still and slow with any movements.

## *Increasing your personal impact exercise*

1. Individually, with video or from feedback, review your approach: are you more king or jester?
2. Don't try too hard (particularly **Sociable**). You never see high-status players trying hard to get things. They may exert effort, but it never seems that way on the outside. Stay cool!
3. No, it's not just a laugh! If you are the butt of all jokes, even if it is funny – you will unconsciously be conveying low status. Avoid it. (Watch out **Sociable** preference.)
4. Be careful not to give up some status to placate others (particularly **Caring**). Changing your behaviour on account of someone else is sometimes appropriate but beware, it can communicate low status.
5. Make a plan and get practising.

Did you know that you are always unconsciously conveying your 'status', and most status-communicating behaviours are hard to fake. One of the best high-status things to learn is Presenter Stance.

## **Presentation Delivery**

There are plenty of topics for discussion when it comes to delivering the presentation. In this book I'll focus on the top three improvement areas for professionals:

1. Presenter Stance.
2. Being constantly aware of the audience.
3. Breathing and voice.

## Presenter Stance

Being confident and being perceived as confident is vital for enhancing your career. Presenter Stance is a good neutral standing posture which makes you feel confident inside and look confident outside.

Presenter stance looks like this:

Aim for this to be your natural resting position and be in this stance most of the time, unless you are consciously doing something else like using your hands appropriately! (See later.)

Those with a **Caring** preference may unconsciously want to be everyone's equal, so may not feel as comfortable with status and owning a room. You may naturally round your shoulders making you smaller, but when presenting you want to be the leader of that group, so you need to stand tall and demonstrate a higher status.

# HIGH PERFORMANCE PRESENTATIONS

Those with a **Sociable** preference may unconsciously try to be the entertainer or joker in the room, so may naturally be more asymmetrical in their body language and make too many fast movements. Focus on straightening up and slowing down.

## How to get into Presenter Stance exercise

1. Before starting your presentation take a few moments to relax and focus on being grounded.
2. Place your feet hip width apart with equal pressure on each foot. Imagine there are tree roots emanating from

each foot to hold you firmly and securely into the floor.
3. Hold your body straight and imagine a string in the centre of your head gently pulling you upright.
    a. In yoga this is similar to the Neutral Spine.
    b. If you hunch over the PC for far too long each day you may want to practise this even more!
4. A fuller description is in my book, 'Taming Your Public Speaking Monkeys'.

Now instead of beginning your presentation on the Downward Spiral, looking nervous and unconfident, you'll begin looking confident, credible and high-status.

## Being constantly aware of the audience

In order to give HPPs, you must be aware of the people around you and flexible enough to adapt – as discussed earlier. You must be switched on enough to notice if something is wrong in the audience and this means being in Peripheral Vision. (Most people are in Peripheral Vision when they are driving i.e. they are aware of everything around them, big picture and not focussed on specific details.) In the context of presenting, the presenter feels and senses the room, meaning if something is said which breaks rapport they will notice a ripple of body language changes or mutterings.

**Information** and **Results** preferences might need to take note especially to improve their awareness of the people in room. For those with a **Caring** preference style, be aware of taking too much notice of the audience, if your monkeys are not 'Tamed', you may be over-concerned about their every move!

## Being constantly aware of the audience exercise

1. Use your Peripheral Vision. (A fuller description of is in my book, 'Taming Your Public Speaking Monkeys'.)
2. Adopt a mindset where you can be aware of how the audience is responding to your communication.
3. When you notice an audience reaction, focus in on the people involved and see what you think their body language is saying.
4. Decide if it is something you (or your body) said or an environmental thing like a sudden draft from a door.
5. Make a decision about how to respond.
    a. If it was something you just said, then you can rescue the situation before it gets out of hand.
    b. Improve your body language or rephrase what you said in a more appropriate way.
    c. Or apologise if it was that bad an error.

Many presenters aren't able to adapt to audience responses in the moment because they aren't aware of them. By using Peripheral Vision you'll understand your environment and continually improve – live.

## Breathing and voice

We tend to help professionals make the most significant improvements in the following areas: improved breathing, slowing down and increasing volume and varying tonality. The first major improvement comes from adopting the Presenter Stance meaning air and breath flows easily in and out of your body whilst preparing, pausing and speaking.

## Improved breathing

We all know how to breathe, don't we? But chances are unless we are musicians, singers, athletes or have completed some presentation skills training, we may not be breathing correctly.

Incorrect breathing contributes to speaking too quickly and can lead to embarrassing gasping or breathlessness. Slow and measured breathing is necessary for good vocal production. Once you've got it right, you'll speak more slowly, project more effectively and you'll feel calmer.

## Breathing exercises

To check you are breathing correctly:
1. Place your hand on your chest (depending on who is looking!) and breathe in. If your hand and rib cage are rising you are breathing incorrectly.
2. Lie down on your back on the floor and put your hand on your tummy and breathe in. Notice how you are breathing correctly now, from your tummy as it rises and falls.
3. Aim to breathe in the same manner when you return to standing. Put your hand on your tummy and breathe with the aim of making your hand rise and fall as you breathe in and out.
4. Prior to going on stage, centre yourself with your breathing; take 3 deep breaths followed by one normal breath.

---
**'Breathing is essential – DON'T STOP!'**
---

## Slowing down

Most presenters (particularly **Results** and **Sociable**) could benefit from slowing down because:

1. It helps them to breathe correctly, thus feel relaxed and calm rather than flustered.
2. It allows time for the audience to ponder what they are saying, digest it and apply it to themselves.
3. It gives them more time – to read the audience and adapt, consider their SAS or prepare questions etc.

Of course, if you are speaking to an international audience you really will want to slow down as well as pause frequently; they have at least one or more additional step(s) in understanding – they need to hear, translate, then apply what they have heard. When I delivered training to a group of European trainers at Toyota in Brussels I had a visual, on the desk in front of me, which said S-l-o-w d-o-w-n to remind me!

## How to slow down exercise

1. Regulate your speed by regulating your breathing.
    a. If you start talking quickly, take a deep breath in through your nose and out through your mouth, then a normal breath, and continue.
    b. If you're wearing a microphone, do it quietly – you don't want to sound like Darth Vader!
    c. Disguise this action if you want to, by taking a moment to take a (quiet) sip of water.
2. Take purposeful pauses – this gives you a chance to think and the audience a chance to process your points. Think of your presentation as a book: as you talk,

picture and imagine where the punctuation would be and pause appropriately.
3. If you have a tendency to mumble, then begin to practise exaggerating how you move your lips when you speak. You want the audience to understand every word you are saying, and that means being deliberate in articulating each sound.
4. Practise – with a buddy (in the actual room, in advance if possible). Ask them to give you feedback on your tone, volume and pace. If you don't have a buddy handy, record yourself to gain an idea of what you sound like, and see where you can improve. Use technology like apps to help you speak more slowly:
    a. Many metronome apps are free. You could set this to the pace at which you normally talk, then slow it down and practise talking to that slower pace. (Some people need to slow down to half their speed!)
    b. At the time of publishing, an app called 'The Speech Pacesetter' was good. You can add your own text, so you can add and practise your actual talk. See my 'apps' blog for more details on this.
5. It's likely that you will speed up when you present for real, so practise being even slower than you need to be.

## Increasing volume and appropriate intonation

### Increasing Volume

The biggest issue tends to be speaking too softly (most often **Caring** and **Information** preferences). This means you may come across as inaudible or meek, so the focus will be here. If you are too loud (most often **Results** and **Sociable** preferences) that may come across as abrasive or annoying – adjust accordingly.

Adopting the Presenter Stance when you present is the first improvement that will mean you can breathe and speak more easily. In addition to that, if you have an opportunity to use a microphone, do so. I used to say I don't need one, but now if it's there I'll use it, because it is easier on your voice and allows the audience to pick up on the finer voice variations you make. When telling a story, you can whisper to suggest, *'I'm telling you a secret'* which isn't easy without a microphone, for example.

### *Volume exercise*

1. Ask a buddy to give you honest feedback, ideally in the room you'll be presenting in.
2. Ensure your breathing is correct.
3. Use a microphone.
    a. Ask for a lapel microphone so your hands are free. Wear something it can be attached to and avoid things that might knock it e.g. necklaces.
    b. For handheld microphones, hold them in line with your mouth, initially 'glued' to the base of your chin, to ensure it moves with your head.
    c. If there's a lectern microphone, if at all possible, bend or pull it to the side so you can then stand to the side of the lectern (not hidden behind it).
    d. Practise where you can stand in relation to the speakers to avoid feedback.

e. Ensure you know how to turn it on/off.

Ultimately, you'll want to adapt your speed, tone and volume to the audience and the story you are telling. Tap into a mix of your Presenter Personality Styles to do that.

***Appropriate intonation***

You may be wondering how something as small as intonation can impact your performance – read on to find out!

In the UK, statements are normally said with neutral or falling intonation. (If you think about reading this sentence it might go down at the end.) In our heads, that falling intonation suggests the end of something i.e. a statement or thought.

Questions are normally said with a rising intonation. (As you read this question, can you hear your voice going up at the end?)

Most people are not aware of this, and that's not usually an issue unless their pitch goes up at the end of most sentences. This may be due to an accent (for example, Australian or New Zealand) or possibly because they just copied someone who did that. When I worked with Jacob's Creek and spent a lot of time with Australian colleagues, people mentioned that I had an Australian twang to my voice – it wasn't intentional, and I thought it was quite fun.

**Females**, **Sociable** and **Caring** especially beware, but all be warned! If you do go up at the end of most of your sentences it impacts your credibility because unconsciously the listener thinks you are unsure of yourself (because you are asking questions most of the time).

A downward intonation for a statement is more commanding, and thus the (UK) audience will find it more believable. I assume this is universal, as no international audiences have mentioned otherwise, but let me know your thoughts after you've completed this exercise.

## *Intonation exercise*

1. Using a downward intonation at the end of this sentence ... say 'We will have this on shelf by 31st July'.
2. Now use an upward intonation instead ... 'We will have this on shelf by 31st July'.
3. Notice that the upward intonation led to the statement being weaker and, as a result, doubt will form in the listener's mind.
4. Most people with a majority upward intonation are not aware they are doing it. Check by recording yourself reading 1 & 2 above and listen out for the appropriate upward and downward movements.
5. If you need to practise going down at the end of your sentences, you'll find it best to get a buddy to help you.
6. Even if you don't usually go up in sentences, you may notice yourself doing so when you are unsure. Practise using the right intonations where appropriate.

This seemingly simple change can make a huge difference to your perceived credibility.

Appropriate presentation delivery is critical to giving HPPs. Without it you risk having your message missed, fading into the background or not being seen as credible enough. But improving your presentation delivery means you'll command the room, inspire others and increase your influencing ability.

## *Conveying information visually*

Communicating visually is so powerful yet in our experience it is, in most organisations, one of the most underutilised skills.

### Why are visuals important?

Using visuals in your presentation is a really important skill to bring to create engaging, persuasive and inspiring presentations. When used well, visuals add impact, reinforce key points and engage the audience. It's obvious we are tuned into visual messages, because a brand logo is often a visual and look how much time and money we invest in getting those seen!

If you are in any way artistic or creative you have the upper hand here, because many of us have lost touch with our visual skills. Remember when you were younger you drew loads of things? What happened? Well perhaps along the way to 'growing up' you stopped using those skills and turned to written communications instead. (After all email doesn't easily allow us to draw concepts does it?) So, I'm going to ask you to re-engage with your visual part of your brain in order to get amazing results!

Interestingly generation wise, Millennials and younger are largely considered to be highly visual because they use Facebook, Instagram, photos, selfies, video, infographics etc. With 50% of the workforce forecast to be Millennials or younger by 2020, we need to get visualising!

Graphics can be used to make information easier to interpret and understand, and to draw attention to important elements. It is therefore especially important to visualise complicated concepts.

For now, let's keep an open mind as to what medium we will use to show the visuals. (You might automatically assume you should use PowerPoint but you could also use your hands, a flip chart, a picture or a video!) Read on and decide on your medium later.

## What type of visual representations should I use?

There are lots of options when it comes to how to convey information visually, for example:

**Graphs** make data easier to read and process. There are plenty to choose from like Bar Charts, Pie Charts, Gantt Charts, Tables, Diagrams, Decision Trees, Organizational Charts, Pyramids,

Timelines. The list is endless. For example, Venn diagrams are good for illustrating how groups work together. You might use a chart to show data, or a pyramid to illustrate key concepts.

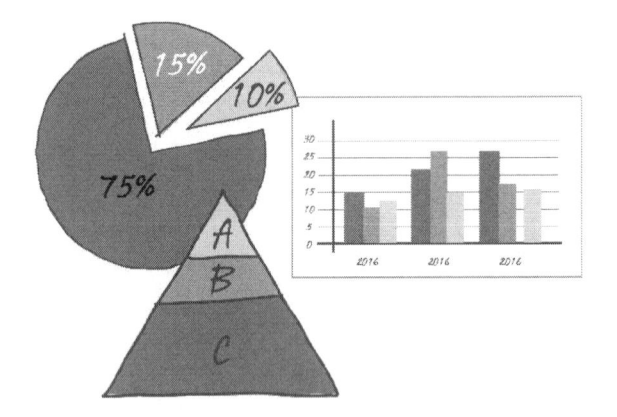

**Illustrations or cartoons** are useful because they can exaggerate points you want to make. (Always ensure you have the usage rights for images or have them drawn for you.)

**Photos or videos** are very powerful tools – keep them short.

**Quotes** – there are plenty of online tools to make quotes into visuals which will bring your point home.

**Symbols** – you might simplify things by choosing to represent something with a symbol. In my first book instead of always writing 'Pubic Speaking Monkeys', I used the symbol @(0_0)@.

**Colours** – Too many people overlook colour when creating visuals. Be aware that green signals go, red equals stop, and amber is neither good nor bad. Use colours consistently. If your brand colour is orange, use orange in your bar charts and graphs. With lighter colours, ensure information is still readable. Use keylines for example, to define areas.

**Drawing** – If you like a challenge, don't overlook drawing something yourself (where appropriate). This may sound scary, but simple illustrations or cartoons can communicate a lot. If you are brave enough to draw live on a flip chart, the audience will be very impressed by, and engaged by, your efforts. They won't be judging you on your artistic competence.

**Timelines** – In the Western world we read from left to right, so we have a sense that time travels from left to right (not right to left). So, in countries where we read from left to right, something in the past is generally placed on the left of the page, and something representing the future is on the right of the page. Obvious right?

2018 — Jan-Mar — Apr-Jun — Jul-Sep — Oct-Dec — 2019 →

✓

But did you know that almost every single one of our clients, before they work with us, are unconsciously doing this wrong when they use their hands! Read about Hands (next) to find out why!

← 2019 — Oct-Dec — Jul-Sep — Apr-Jun — Jan-Mar — 2018

✗

## How to improve your visual representations exercise

1. Whether you are using PowerPoint or not in your

presentation, refer to Smart Art on PowerPoint to get ideas of how you can use different visuals to clearly communicate your point.
2. Be consistent with your visuals, for example, as above, if you use colours or symbols then keep those consistent throughout the presentation AND for future presentations too.
3. Keep your visuals simple. Use one visual concept for one point. Don't over complicate visuals with anything unnecessary – strip it back to essentials.
4. Variety – If you often share the same message e.g. at weekly meetings, vary the way you deliver it. Consider stories, testimonials, poems, props, quizzes etc.
5. Location, location, location – As you become more advanced in your skills, you'll want to learn and understand more about location and what it conveys to the audience. The most common location skill we teach clients about is timelines because they are so powerful, useful and far-reaching.

## Hands

Hands are Mother Nature's PowerPoint. We are meant to use them to communicate. The problem comes when people are careless with their hands and let them talk too much!

> **Don't babble with your hands!**

I often tell clients to keep their hands still by their side until they know what to do with them, otherwise they may be giving out the wrong message with their hands.

Why? Because you are a mirror image of the audience when

you present, everything is back to front. That's one of the reasons we say to clients, *'If you don't know what you are doing with your hands keep them still until you do'*!

> **Like the Hippocratic Oath, first do no harm!**
>
> **If you don't know what you are doing with your hands keep them still until you do!**

## How to improve your hands and gestures

The safest place for your hands is by your side, until you know what to do with them.

### *Minimising your hands exercise*

I suggest you practise using no hands (or very minimal hands) by filming yourself. Try this:

1. Aim to speak easily for a minute or two without moving your hands from your side.
2. If you notice yourself using your hands, ask yourself is that a helpful movement for the audience or a hindrance? As my comedy tutor used to say, *'If it doesn't add it distracts'*.
3. If your hand movement is not useful to the audience, then stop it and keep your hands by your side until you can use them usefully.
4. If you think your hand movement is useful then study it and ensure you do it correctly, consciously and clearly.
5. Once you've decided on unique hand movements to represent key messages then practise the gestures in the right place in the presentation until it is second nature.

### *Creating effective hand movements*

Ensure your hand movements are correct, conscious and clear:

**Correct** – make sure it's the correct way round for your audience. For example, in the HOW let's say you want to you talk through an action plan with timescales. If you indicate January is the start you'll want the audience to see that on the left and December, the end, should be on the right. Do that now with your hands. What most people will find is that they have their left hand out for January and their right hand out for December. That's right. For you! But the presentation isn't about you, it's about the audience. So in fact, because you are a mirror image to the audience, you'll need to do what feels backwards to you and start with your right hand for January and end on your left hand for December.

In another example you might be talking about the competitor's product; you'll want to indicate unconsciously with your hands that it is in the past (right hand) and your company's new product is in the future (left hand).

**Conscious** means do it on purpose. Plan to have one unique hand movement representing one key point. (That also means you wouldn't need a PowerPoint to represent that same point as well.) Every time you repeat that key point you'd want to re-use that unique hand movement to 'land' the message.

*Examples of good hand movements:*

Hands are great for counting your 3 points on especially your 3 WHAT sections. I tend to use the thumb for point 1, first finger for point 2 and second finger for point 3. This keeps me out of trouble, avoiding random flying round of offensive fingers!

If you wanted to use your hands to convey a Venn diagram, each party would be represented by each hand. Bring them together to show the cross over and harmony as they work together well.

You want your body language to match your words and not contradict what you are saying. When you are talking about trust and group working, you don't want your body screaming 'defensive' without even realising it. (Having your arms crossed in front of you may be obviously defensive, but did you know palms held together, or grasped protecting your private parts, are also gestures suggesting self-protection?)

A professional speaker recently confessed to a specific hand movement he made which was inadvertently offensive in another culture. If you are crossing culture, research your desired hand movements in advance!

**Clear** is all about making sure that if you use hand movements, they are clear to people watching. If it's a large audience, you'll need big, bold gestures and ideally away from the body, so the hands can be seen separately from the body not all bunched up. For example, using your hand to draw a line from your tummy button to a meter from your tummy button is not clear because the audience can't see it. Much clearer then is to signal the 'line' to one side of your body or another. And then ensure that it moves in the 'right' direction as discussed earlier!) Once you've finished your hand movement, put your arms back down by your side until it is time for the next correct, conscious and clear hand movement.

> **Hands are like toys: they need to be put away after use.**

In between hand movements keep them down by your side otherwise you're polluting your message. If you aren't ready to use your hands well, keep them still otherwise you risk distracting, confusing or contradicting your message.

### *Creating effective hand movements exercise*

Ensure your hand movements are correct, conscious and clear:

1. Practise using your hands correctly.
    a. Start with your right hand for January and end on your left hand for December for example.
    b. As another exercise draw a timeline on a flip

chart and place it behind you.
  c. Face forward and practise demonstrating that timeline with your hands.
  d. Turnaround to check that your hands are in the same place as the flip chart would suggest they should be.
2. Practise using your hands consciously.
  a. Plan which unique hand movements you will use to represent key points.
  b. Decide which messages will be told with your hands and which, if any, require PowerPoint.
  c. Decide if and where it is appropriate to repeat that same hand movement to reiterate your message.
3. Practise using your hands clearly.
  a. With a buddy or a video, notice your hand movements as you practise your presentation.
  b. Review after to see if your movements were clear and good for the audience.

When you do use your hands well it can help you remember your key points more easily, make it more engaging for the audience and more memorable.

## Using PowerPoint appropriately – as a visual aid

The most common way to present information in the business setting is via a PowerPoint presentation. I'm sure you've had to sit through presentations of this sort and can see how they can become monotonous and even boring. To ensure that your PowerPoint presentation doesn't send the audience to sleep, you need to know how to use PowerPoint slides appropriately, in a manner that adds to your message.

If you want visuals, decide on whether you can use your hands, a flip chart or other medium before defaulting to PowerPoint.

PowerPoint (or Keynote on Mac) is the main software that people turn to, but those with Public Speaking Monkeys often use PowerPoint incorrectly. People with a *'You'll Look Stupid'* Monkey try to avoid looking stupid by having their script written out on PowerPoint. Unfortunately, without meaning to, they can often end up looking stupid. Why? Most people aren't practised at reading out loud, so they may stumble over words. And because they are looking at the 'script', they are not able to engage with the audience or adapt to what's going on in the room. And it goes on and on!

It's a similar story for those with other monkeys. Ironically, their presentation is more likely to go badly because of the very monkey telling them it will go badly.

There are hundreds of articles and illustrations of good vs. bad PowerPoint on the web, as well as specific courses, if you want to explore this more; to follow are some pointers.

## How to improve your visuals exercise

1. Make sure any monkeys are 'Tamed' then, before going anywhere near the computer, create your SAS. Only once you are happy with your SAS should you start to think about visual aids.
2. Look at your SAS and ask yourself which parts of your presentation could benefit from:
    a. Being simplified.
    b. Becoming clearer.
    c. Increased emphasis.
3. Pick up a pen and paper and draw out the appropriate charts – not exactly, but just roughly to visualise the message. Some people are good at this, but most seem

to find it tough to use a visual that makes key points clearer. An example of a good, simple visual is below.

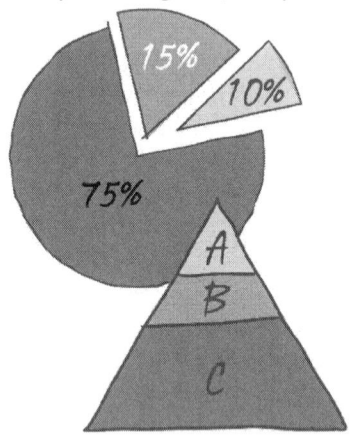

4. Once you have a good visual, then decide if you are going to show it with your hands, on a flip chart, with a leaflet or a slide.
    a. As an exercise in increasing your presenting flexibility, think about how you could communicate your information if no PowerPoint was available. How else could you do to get your message across? e.g. if there were two elements, you could show them visually as arrows on a flip chart, show them as circles with your hands or you might use your hands to show a set of scales to show the balance on both sides of a process.
    b. Consider using flip charts – they are more interactive than PowerPoint as they allow two-way engagement. Between any slides you could gather feedback from the audience.
5. If you don't find visualising easy, ask someone with a more visual mind to help you. Over time you will learn

from them. A great website to visit, to see it done well, is www.informationisbeautiful.net and if you are preparing a very important presentation you may want to employ a professional to help you.

6. Finally, remember it's less about the slides and more about how the slides lead the audience through your talk. Practise with the slides to see how they look.

**How to use PowerPoint exercise**

Follow these Do's & Don'ts of PowerPoint creation and use:

1) Do...

- ✓ Ensure each slide has a purpose or a point.

- ✓ Title slides with the key point you want to make e.g. 'sales declined 15%' – ensure your visual shows that.

- ✓ Be consistent with font styles and sizes, when you choose capitals etc.

- ✓ Develop an in-house style/slide design then stick to it.

- ✓ Put additional slides in the appendix or have them as hidden slides and refer to them if required.

- ✓ Use Smart Art to illustrate systems, thoughts, processes etc. in a visual manner.

- ✓ Always get to the venue early and test the equipment.

- ✓ Preload your presentation and look through every page to spot formatting errors.

- ✓ Make sure your notes (if you need them) are on note

cards, then you can talk to the audience not the screen.

✓ Obvious perhaps, but ensure you're plugged in – it's not great when even your computer falls asleep!

✓ Take a copy of your presentation on a USB stick in case you need to use a different computer.

✓ Increase your stage area by turning the projector beam off when not in use. In Slide Show, press 'B' on the keyboard. Press any key to turn it back on.

✓ Use a remote-control clicker to make slide changing look seamless and free you up from the desk/lectern.

2) Don't...

- ✗ Cram too much information or too many graphs onto a slide. Keep the chart clean (**Information**).

- ✗ Overdo the slide builds, sound effects or animation – that can just get annoying!

- ✗ Be tempted to use the PowerPoint's internal notes function or you'll be staring at the PC, not making eye contact with the audience, and the Downward Spiral will start!

- ✗ Rely solely on the projector – I see it as added value if it all works OK. Always have hard copy for your own reference in case the projector has a hissy fit, or in case the fire alarm goes off and you have to present outdoors!

- ✗ Flick forwards and backwards through your slides. If you are RUNNING slide show on a PC, you can enter the page number of a slide then 'Enter' – to jump to that slide.

- ✗ Don't walk in front of the projector; if the light from the projector is shining in your eyes ... you are in the way of the screen.

3) The start of the presentation is when you create your first impression. Plan ahead and ask yourself how you will ensure you get the technical/equipment issues sorted in advance, so you'll be able to concentrate on giving a great presentation!

There are, of course, other software systems like Prezi that have tried to address some of the classic issues with using PowerPoint. If you are a super techy these might work for you. I still advise pen and paper first!

A lack of awareness of visual tools – either not using them or using them poorly, contributes to Low Performance Presentations. It can mean people don't 'get' the message clearly; the message might fail to filter down the organisation and you could come across as a weak communicator.

A good visual presentation is an opportunity to convey your business message more easily, clearly and succinctly. When you use the tools wisely you will ensure your audience is not only looking at you and the slides, but also digesting the message and considering what they can learn from you.

In this chapter we've looked at personal impact and presentation delivery, and how to communicate visually. In the next chapter we'll cover techniques for engaging and interacting with your audience. But before that, let's look at the third of four 'Success Stories'. Keep an eye out specifically for things we've just covered on tone and stance for example.

## *Success Story – Karen Caring*

*Karen worked within a global technology company and was committed to her job. She started work in the customer care department and did so well there that she was invited to move into a marketing role to utilise her in-depth customer knowledge and understanding. She was surprised to discover she both enjoyed it and was good at it. She consistently scored well on her appraisals and sales colleagues and customers always said how much they liked working with her, because she listened to their needs and addressed issues fairly. Her team were loyal and tight knit, and staff turnover was low. Her style order preference was* **Caring, Information, Sociable, Results.**

*Karen had worked in marketing for 6 years, but despite her boss saying she was 'valued and appreciated', the board felt she 'didn't have the gravitas or personal impact' necessary to become a senior manager.*

*Karen wondered how the board could judge her – when they only see her once a month at the review meeting, with 15 other*

*people.*

*Karen's boss recommended she work with 'Simply Amazing Training' on a one-to-one basis to work on her executive presence. After Karen spoke to us she got the feeling that, with help, she could do a lot more in those monthly meetings to demonstrate her competence, even though she felt she shouldn't have to.*

*Her mentor worked with Karen to uncover any monkeys – turns out she had a 'You Don't Fit In' Monkey (left from school days when she moved from Ireland to London and was teased for her accent). She had forgotten all about that and was stunned to see that it was still impacting her behaviours to this day. It was feeding the behaviour of 'not standing out' and 'not wanting to put herself forward too much for fear of being ridiculed'. After taming the monkey, she worked with her mentor to develop more helpful mindsets, skillsets and toolsets.*

*Karen particularly benefitted from the following:*

- *Working on her visibility in the meetings. She didn't want to be one of those people who just spoke for the sake of it, but she began to see the importance of speaking up more. When she was happy with her presentation content, she practised presenter stance to convey gravitas (instead of making herself as small as possible and not even wanting to stand up). She particularly loved our tip, that to convey status in a meeting, she could stand up more often, and visualising things on the flip chart was a great excuse to do this!*

- *Karen was softly spoken so she worked on improving*

her volume and quality of tone. With her old monkey, despite knowing she should speak louder, she never would have, but now she is free to practise and do so. She kept her friendly approach and her language still has a caring bias, but she has added a touch of directness to get her message across more strongly.

- She loved every part of the SAS, and for her the HOW section needed the most work. In her previous presentations she'd rarely even had a HOW section; she worked with her mentor to have a really clear HOW, and be strong and direct in asking for what she wanted, i.e. support for her team, and for others to buy into her new approach. They also honed in on conveying her strategic thinking in her presentations to demonstrate her suitability for a senior role.

Karen successfully adapted her style to her surroundings. The changes made a dramatic difference - her boss and the board could 'see' her quality of contribution more easily now. Within just a few months she was added to the 'secret' high-potential leaders list!

# Chapter 11
# High Performance Presentations are interactive, interesting and inspiring

*How to be interactive, interesting and inspiring*

There are hundreds of tips on making presentations engaging – I want to cover the three areas I've seen to be most relevant for business professionals today:

- Replacing one-way presentations with two-way communications makes them interactive and automatically more interesting. (**All styles** especially **Information** and **Results**.)
- Telling stories in a business context engages the brain to make messages more interesting and inspiring. (**All styles** especially **Information, Results** and **Caring**.)
- Making conference calls engaging – by using the above techniques and other call tips. (**All Styles**.)

## Make it a two-way conversation

Many presentations are boring because they are more like a one-way lecture and less like a two-way conversation we might enjoy every day. One of the secrets to an engaging presentation is to make it more conversational, and questions help do this. But, if you've seen people attempt questions in their presentations before and they've crashed into a stony wall of silence you may be a bit cautious! Fair enough! Would it be OK then if I were to show you how to ask questions effectively?

## Use open and closed questions appropriately

You know what closed questions are, don't you? Closed questions are questions that have a specific short answer, like yes or no; whereas open questions open up the conversation. Open questions do not have a black and white answer – it is shades of grey or matters of opinion that form the answer.

### *Examples of closed questions*

Q: *'Does that make sense?'*

A: *Yes/no*

Q: *'Can we get the product ready for 15th March delivery?'*

A: *Yes/no*

They encourage a wrong/right, yes/no style of answer.

Closed questions are great for:

- Getting a direct and short answer.
- Confirming details.
- Closing off discussions.

In contrast, they are not good for:

- Encouraging discussion.
- Continuing conversation.
- Opening up new avenues of thought and new ideas.

### Examples of open questions

Q: 'What topic makes the most sense to you?'

A: 'I liked the section on rapport because ...'

Q: 'What do we need to do to get the product ready for delivery on the 15th March?'

A: 'We will need to order the widgets today to get them here in time, which might cost more.'

Open questions are great for:

- Gathering people's thoughts and opinions.
- Checking there are no unstated objections.
- Gaining buy-in to ideas.

Open questions are not so great for:

- Giving specific directions on what you want. (E.g. 'Any questions' is not as clear as, 'Do you have any questions on section 1?')
- Gaining commitment to specific actions. (E.g. 'What actions might you take now?' may not be as clear as a closed question like, 'Who thinks they can show this to the customer in the next week?')
- Wrapping up conversations or closing down decisions.

## Where to use questions in the SAS

Closed and open questions can be used throughout the SAS.

In the LITTLE INTRO section of your talk, you might want to use closed questions to get an idea of the levels of knowledge on your topic before you start.

For example, if you are presenting the quarterly figures and you want to get an idea of the level of knowledge in the room (so you can adapt your presentation accordingly) you might say, *'Before we start, has anyone here already seen the final figures for this year?'* (Nod and put your hand up, which indicates to the audience they need to answer with a nod and a hand up.) Then follow that with, *'Great, thank you'* or something similar, to praise the audience's good behaviour. This also sets the bar for future responses you expect.

You may want to open a presentation in the LITTLE INTRO with a question around thoughts and feelings so far, and only then move on to the next stage. This gives you a heads-up that either you are on the right track and you have paced the audience well – they are where you are on the topic – or that you haven't paced them so well – they feel differently to what you thought or new information may have come to light that you were unaware of.

For example, you might ask, *'Before we begin, I'd like to just capture some of your thoughts around this project so far. What is your thinking and understanding of where we are in the process at this moment?'* This gives you the chance to adapt what you are about to say to the audience rather than charging in like a bull, and only finding out at the very end that they aren't with you!

In the WHY section, questions are essential if you want to do the interactive version rather than just the direct approach. Your aim is to predict all possible answers, and then ask the appropriate closed questions to elicit the correct audience responses. For example, *'Who here hates wasting time?'*

You could use open questions to help get buy-in to the WHY section in the SAS structure. For example, *'I'd like to share the latest campaign results with you. Why do you think it might be helpful for you to know this information even if you aren't in marketing?'*

During the WHY section especially, open questions are very helpful in conjunction with a flip chart or white board. In order to maintain rapport, use the same language (words) and replay (audience responses) rather than paraphrase. For example, when eliciting responses verbally or on a flip chart, always use the exact words they have used when you play it back to them or write it down. It is best to plan this as much as you can because, by their very nature, open questions may take a little time.

I especially like using closed questions at the end of each topic in the WHAT section to check the understanding of the previous section, for example, *'Are you now clear on the top 3 reasons why we need to act quickly?'* This kind of question does a number of things.

**Pacing** – it allows you to check in with the audience and see that they are all nodding with you (and if not, to uncover with an open question what they need in order to be with you).

**Consolidation** – the question itself consolidates the key point of the topic or section you just finished.

**Engagement** – when an audience member listens and nods along to your questions they feel part of the discussion. These closed questions are an essential part of the difference between a boring presentation, where the audience feel talked at, and an interesting presentation, where the audience feel they have been part of a 2-way interaction or conversation.

In the WHAT section there may be less open questioning depending on the topic, as the WHAT section in a presentation tends to be more of an information giving session. Having said that, you might want to use appropriate open questions to gain buy-in, for example at the end of WHAT 1, 2 and 3.

In the HOW section it is important, once you know what next steps need to be taken, that you get agreement from the people taking the action that they will do it. The process of asking the audience to agree and nod with you gets them to consider and then answer the question for themselves in their head, thus increasing commitment.

If you are working with a larger audience, a closed question can help you do this quite quickly. For example, *'The next step is to go online and vote before Friday. Can you find just 5 minutes in your diary to do that?'* (Of course, the smaller the ask, the more likely you'll get agreement, which is one of the reasons it can be better to break big asks into chunks or separate presentations over time, rather than expecting too much from one presentation.)

The HOW section is just perfect for open questions if you want to gain buy-in to those action points and next steps. If there is not a clear path to what should be done next, then it is great to use open questions to pull together a team action plan. For example, in a departmental meeting where you are wanting to allocate tasks out to others you might say, *'So what are the next best steps to make this happen?'* Be aware that the discussion and action plan still need managing – you don't want chaos to ensue!

As you ask the questions you need to be flexible, have some idea of the direction you want to go in and by allowing some new avenues to be explored that you've not thought of, you may well get some of the best solutions. Also, the more people are involved and come up with the action steps themselves, the more ownership they will have of taking the actions.

In the HOW section, for example of a conference speech, you might intend to get the audience to experience the learning point for themselves and get them relating it to their own day-to-day role. You may give them an open question to discuss with a buddy sitting next to them:

*'In a moment, when I say go, I'm going to ask you to pair up with a person next to you. Take 2 minutes to discuss the following question: 'How could you use this new knowledge in your day-to-day role?' I will then ask for a few volunteers to share their thoughts with the room.'*

The WHAT IF section starts with an open question: *'What Questions and Thoughts do you have?'* and of course the audience may be asking open or closed questions.

If someone asks a big and open question you might be tempted to over explain (**Information** and **Caring**). My advice here would be to answer the question in as few sentences as you can, to do a reasonable job. Then stop and ask a closed question to the person who asked you, *'Does that answer your question, or would you like more information?'* That way you can judge the level of detail given and manage time effectively. You could always take the rest of the discussion offline if one person needs a lot more detail than others.

In the WHAT IF section, you could also encourage further discussion by adding in a subsequent open question such as, *'What do you think will be the fastest approach?'* or *'How do you think the competition will respond?'* For more information on answering questions you could revisit Chapter 8.

## How to ensure the audience answer your questions

Asking the audience to get involved is great assuming the situation is appropriate, but people have often had bad experiences of questions falling on deaf ears. Here's how to ask questions and get the audience responding. (Yes, even British audiences will respond if you follow these points!)

## *Be aware of the audience's feelings and preferences*

- ✓ Build rapport with your audience first to get them engaged (**Results** and **Information** especially take note).
- ✓ Introverted preference audience members particularly prefer being given advance notice of what is to come e.g. *'In a few moments I'm going to ask you to go around the room, from left to right and ask you to give me your thoughts ...'* (**Results** and **Sociable** take note).
- ✓ Wait for answers, especially from more introverted preference audience members (**Results** and **Sociable** especially take note). They need time to think. Wait for at least 10 seconds, which will seem like an especially long time for the extroverted preference types.
- ✓ For sensitive topics you need to build trust – for example, when speaking about the fear of speaking I can't just ask, *'What are you scared of?'* as people will feel uncomfortable answering. You can either tell your own story here, and open up to the audience, or tell a story of someone you've worked with who has suffered terribly. For example, one lady used to faint before presenting. This is true – and all of a sudden someone's red face and sweaty palms don't seem so bad! (**Results** and **Information** especially take note.)
- ✓ Many people hate answering questions because to them it is public speaking (they have their own Public Speaking Monkeys). You can make it easier for them by:
  - Working in pairs or small groups to discuss the

question. Then you can ask those who are comfortable to feed back.
- Giving out Post-It Notes and asking the audience to write their answer on the Post-It Note and then stick it on a wall.

✓ Use the answers you get. Weave the answers they give into the flow of your presentation and adapt your content accordingly. Otherwise the audience may wonder what the point of contributing was (**Results** and **Information** especially take note).

✓ Writing up the answers on the flip chart also demonstrates that you value the audience's answers.
- If the answers are coming very fast, you may need to have an assistant to help you write them up.
- Write them up, as closely as you can, to the way the person said them.
- If you need to paraphrase, check with the person that it accurately reflects what they said.

✓ Do not embarrass anyone. You may think that you would never do this, but it's incredibly easy to do unintentionally (**Results** and **Information** take note). Here's how to avoid doing it:
- Acknowledge each answer you get and don't favour a specific answer (because others may feel rejected in comparison).
- If somebody's answer is totally wrong or misguided, take responsibility for it. For example, you might say, *'Oh! That's not quite what I was looking for, but I can see why you said that. What I meant was ...'*

✓ **Results** and **Sociable**, be careful when calling on very strongly introverted preference types to answer off the cuff without preparation.

## *Give the audience clarity and guidance*

- ✓ Make your questions simple and clear – they won't answer if they are not 100% clear on what the questioner really wants as an answer (**Sociable** and **Caring** take note).
- ✓ If you are looking for specific answers, you can demonstrate to the audience the type of answer you are looking for by giving an example.
- ✓ Start asking questions early on so the audience realise that interaction is expected.
- ✓ Ask clarification questions at the end of each mini section in the SAS, where appropriate.
- ✓ Tell people how you want them to answer before asking the question. Sometimes people don't answer a question because they don't know what you want them to do – give them a heads-up.
- ✓ Avoid mixing rhetorical questions (these are questions you don't expect your audience to answer) with 'real' questions. Your audience will get confused about whether they're supposed to answer or not.
- ✓ If nobody answers, you could repeat the question and ask them to talk to their neighbour about it, or give the answer yourself and move on smoothly with your presentation. (**Caring** don't take this personally or let it put you off asking other questions in the future.)

## *Techniques and tips for experienced presenters*

- ✓ If you have a big room you can ask people to get physically involved in the answer which brings energy

to the presentation too – great after breaks. (**Results** and **Information** especially take note.) For example, I use this technique for people to see the level of presenting experience in the room. I'll stand at one end of the line and say, *'Stand here if you've got lots of experience presenting'*, then I'll walk down the line to about the half-way spot and say, *'Stand here if you've got some experience'* and then down to the other end and say, *'Stand here if you've got less experience'*. After they've lined up, speak to people and ask why they have positioned themselves there (if appropriate).
- ✓ After the presentation, ask for a Feedback Sandwich (see my first book) from individual audience members.
- ✓ **Caring** and **Information**, manage the situation if someone (often with a **Sociable** preference) hogs the limelight. If after other efforts to stop them talking fails, you could say calmly, *'Thanks and I need to move on now to …'* and then take a question elsewhere.
- ✓ To increase compliance, ask the audience to all raise their hands and then say, *'Now, drop your hand if…'* rather than asking them to *'Raise your hand if…'*.

## Two-way presentations exercise

1. Go through your final SAS to see where you can add engagement and interactivity.
2. Identify specifically where you can add in appropriate conversational open and closed questions.
3. Practise asking those questions and anticipate answers.
4. You don't have to wait until a presentation to ask these questions – practise in daily conversations.
5. Test out questions on colleagues to see if you get the responses you want before the big day (**Results** and **Sociable** especially take note).

Now you know how to ask questions effectively let's look at adding interest by telling stories, and before your monkeys say 'You *can't tell stories*' read on and you'll see you already do!

## Telling stories in a business context

Why use a story? Neurologists say that our brains are programmed much more for stories than for abstract ideas. Case studies, testimonials, or product benefits told as stories, with a little drama, are remembered far longer than any slide crammed with data and bullet points.

Many great stories (and even some not-so-great jokes) have been structured using the magic number 3. Think of 'Goldilocks and the Three Bears', 'The Three Little Pigs', and 'Three Blind Mice'. The story is also then split into 3: a beginning, middle and end. You can use the magic number in SAS, to introduce your background and problems, then reveal the solution you have to overcome it and finish off with evidence or a vision of the future. Within the story you could repeat your 3 key points using the same words, phrases or visuals – repetition aids retention.

If your story has a reason to be in the presentation (to help the audience) and it is succinct then it's probably a good thing. Let's dive into more detail on the power of case studies.

## Case Studies

Stories, especially case studies, help with subtle persuasion. A case study is a story, and they are great for persuading people because as humans we love social proof. If done well, using case studies is a great way to showcase what you can do and to get audience engagement. Often, they can form a great third part in the 'WHAT' section. (**Information** and **Results** preference take special note.)

Stories are great at helping you to take a more subtle approach (a skill for **Results** and **Information** preferences to note!) When you say things in a direct manner, the audience/listener is likely to be aware of what you are doing e.g. telling them how good the product is, selling to them, etc.

With well-crafted stories you may be indirectly suggesting how good the product is or why they should buy from you but it is more subtle, more likely to maintain rapport and thus decrease objections.

For example, when I'm talking about the work we do at Simply Amazing Training, I could say:

*'Working with us is great because we help people improve their presentation skills and thus their careers.'*

But telling a story is likely to be much more engaging:

*John was confident in his abilities, he was well liked, intelligent and a great negotiator; but when it came to internal presentations he became robotic, lost his personality and became short of breath.*

*When he worked with us, he was surprised he enjoyed the process and was delighted with the results. Now he is calm, confident and relaxed, meaning he can breathe easily, engage others and bring his personality to his presentations.*

*That was three years ago. Now he enjoys presenting and seeks out opportunities to speak which has raised his profile and according to him was a major factor in his recent successes.*

## Creating a case study exercise

1. Choose a case study that your audience will associate with. It should tell a story, rather than be only data-driven, because stories are more memorable.
2. Make sure the story flows easily and has a point. Use a Before, During and After scenario to demonstrate how you helped, i.e. the situation before you helped (how

bad it was), the solution you provided during the time they worked with you (e.g. how easy it was to work with you) and finally the situation after they worked with you (e.g. how successful they are now).
3. Talk on an emotional level wherever possible. This will immerse listeners.
4. Avoid industry jargon – explain everything (succinctly) even if it's obvious to you.
5. End on a positive note highlighting how you helped the customer/situation.
6. If you have permission from a client to tell their story, use real names and exact figures (if it doesn't risk confidentiality).
   a. The case study is even more believable if it's in their words.
   b. If they are short on time, talk to them on the phone and transcribe the conversation.
   c. If possible, take the story one step on. For example, if you saved your client £2,100 per month, find out what they are doing with that money now. You might be able to say, *'With the £2,100 a month we saved our client, they were able to employ another member of staff.'*
   d. Ask to use a photo of them and add that in to make it even more real, or even better, get them on video telling the story themselves!

When presenting it is important you come across as credible, but no one likes a show off! Generally, in my observation, being comfortable saying you are good is a more masculine trait, and a more feminine trait is being coy or reserved about abilities or successes, even to yourself. Maybe this is because, from a young age, women in the UK are not encouraged to show off, yet if a boy scores a goal in football they are encouraged to yell, jump and pull their shirts over their heads!

My view is it's all about intention – are you doing it to say how good you are? Or is it important to be credible so you can inspire others? Many women, and some men, need to find their own way to be comfortable (within their Presenter Personality Style) demonstrating their expertise for the benefit of the audience. Well told stories about your past successes can build credibility in a subtle way. (**Caring** types take special note to create credibility – you'll probably find the case study approach more comfortable.)

## Where to use stories in the SAS

Stories can be used anywhere within your SAS.

Little INTRO and WHY – At the beginning you could include short stories like:

- ✓ How the company/product started e.g. 'When I was asked to work with young children, I needed a way to communicate what I knew in a simple, fun and effective manner. That's when the two wooden monkeys from my Mum and Dad came to mind.'
- ✓ Short story illustrating a WHY e.g. 'Last week I was talking to Bob who mentioned his sales weren't as high as he wanted.'

WHAT – In your WHAT section you could include:

- ✓ Case studies and customer testimonials.
- ✓ How to use the product.
- ✓ What happens when you implement the ideas.
- ✓ How you got to be passionate about X.
- ✓ How the product/service/idea came to be born.
- ✓ Personal or company history (where relevant).
- ✓ A typical client who used to have the 'problem'.
- ✓ A typical client who implemented your 'solution'.
- ✓ A typical client, three years after using your service.

HOW and WHAT IF – You could tell stories that:
- ✓ Show how easily someone else found it to take action.
- ✓ Help the audience understand what to expect, e.g. a time when you went outside your comfort zone.

## Add stories to your SAS exercise

1. Review your SAS and see where you could replace drier messages with a story that would get that same point across but in a more engaging manner.
2. Take time to create good stories – you'll find it easy to repeat and reuse them, even in daily conversations.
3. If you want your teams to use the same story – make sure the topic is universal enough for them to be able to tell it themselves congruently. For example, stories about good and bad customer service are likely to be fairly generic, but stories about your specific teacher when you grew up are not!

Advanced Tip:

Nancy Duarte is great at stories. I recommend reading her blog, 'Improve Your Storytelling Presentation Skills and Get Your

Ideas Adopted', her book, 'Resonate' and her TED talks, particularly 'The Secret Structure of Great Talks'.

## Metaphors and similes

Metaphors and similes are great for simplifying messages. Both similes and metaphors are used to describe one thing in terms of another in order to make them come to life or be understood more easily – however they do so differently. A simile uses 'like' or 'as' in the comparison. A metaphor says something is something else. I'm not too worried about the definitions but more how to use them.

For example, I say, *'Think of your presentation as a book ... at the end of each sentence, take a short pause, to let the ideas sink in. At the end of each paragraph, take a longer pause.'*

Metaphors and similes are great for making complex ideas simple. The trick is to compare the thing you are explaining to something that is easy to understand and regarded as a positive (if that's your objective).

Steve Jobs used similes in his speeches – *'Same as a BlackBerry'*, *'It [multitouch] works like magic'* and *'Now, software on mobile phones is like baby software.'*

## Metaphor and similes exercise

1. Get your brain into the right mode – take some time out for a moment, don't think about a 'right' answer, just let your unconscious mind open up.
2. Answer the following:
    a. The product is small and compact – it's like

b. The system is so fast and responsive like
      _____

   c. _____ is like wading
      through treacle.

3. If this isn't natural you can learn to improve. Google has plenty of ideas on how to do that.

The final area I've noticed all styles can benefit from is improving the engagement levels on conference calls. I'm using this as a generic term for a multitude of programmes, systems or apps where people talk and even see one another remotely.

## Making conference calls engaging – yes, it's possible!

Conference calls or video calls need even more preparation to be engaging, and everything you've learned in the book so far applies and more! Your job is to make it easy to listen because on a conference call you have no (or less) body language to add to your message, making listening more difficult – because we speak at 125 to 250 words per minute but think at 1000 to 3000 words per minute.

On a conference call, engage the listener all the way through the presentation by making it a two-way conversation – ask for hands up or comments in the dialogue box or use tag questions (see advanced skills in the next chapter).

Be mindful that the WHY and engaging the listeners is even more important. People need to quickly know the benefits of listening (not reading their emails!) and they need to be kept engaged throughout. When hundreds of people are on a conference call, they can wonder what they are doing there.

The WHAT is even more important because without a clear structure the listener gets lost quickly. You may benefit from breaking your SAS into even smaller chunks than you would face-to-face. It may be better to have several calls with more bespoke audiences than trying to cover everything in one call.

In the HOW section, ensure people have committed to their action/deadlines rather than assuming they have.

For the WHAT IF, you need to manage questions well – perhaps have a second helper who can manage and group questions while you answer others.

## Conference call tips:

*Getting ready*

- ✓ Invite your participants with plenty of notice (**Results** and **Sociable** preference take note).
- ✓ Issue an agenda with topics in plenty of time (**Results** and **Sociable** preference).
- ✓ Encourage participants to do the relevant preparation.
- ✓ Check your WiFi connection, speakerphone volume and software.
- ✓ Include instructions on how to make the call (**Results** and **Sociable** preference).
- ✓ Tell participants if they need to have anything prepared or facts to hand (**Results** and **Sociable** preference).
- ✓ Choose a quiet environment away from air conditioning, printers, ringing phones, etc.
- ✓ Ask to be made aware of any important issues well

before the call.
- ✓ Call in early, especially if you are host (**Results** and **Sociable** preference).

***Beginning and during the call***
- ✓ Identify yourself when you start using a powerful greeting, so the audience are attentive and receptive.
- ✓ Stick to the agenda – use note cards as prepared in the SAS, with each point you need to cover on a separate card and stack them in order. Flip through the cards as topics are covered. Take notes on the back of the card if necessary (**Results** and **Sociable** preference).
- ✓ Give participants clear instructions and session agreements.
- ✓ Request participants wait until after the call to answer emails or send texts.
- ✓ Praise punctuality.

- ✓ Encourage people to use the mute button when not speaking to reduce background noise.
- ✓ Remind participants to state their name before speaking or answering questions.
- ✓ State which meeting everyone is in.
- ✓ Let them know the expected length of the session.
- ✓ Review the objective of the meeting, format and agenda (**Results** and **Sociable** preference).
- ✓ Don't let anyone take you off topic/agenda (**Caring** preference). To help, set up a 'car park' concept where you take topics to one side into a virtual car park. Then discuss the issue/question at the end or separately.
- ✓ Stick to time – people may have booked meetings to follow your call.
- ✓ Encourage interaction – ask participants for their thoughts using comments, polls, virtual hands up etc.
- ✓ Make sure what you are saying matches the appropriate visual at the right time.
- ✓ Vary the tone of your voice, to match the 'story' you are telling. A monotone voice (**Information** preference beware) can bore the audience on a conference call.
- ✓ Use your energy and passion, projected through your voice, to help keep people engaged.
- ✓ If you have an accent or talk quickly (**Results** and **Sociable** preference) slow down more than normal.
- ✓ Stay in the moment with all participants, all of the time.
- ✓ Address people by name – they'll pay closer attention if they think they might be called upon for their input.

### *At the end of the call*
- ✓ When ending the call, encourage others to recap the main points/actions of the meeting (**Results** and **Sociable** preference).
- ✓ Ask specific closed questions. Refrain from asking, *'Does anyone have a question?'* Say, *'What are your thoughts on X?'* or, *'Share your comments about Y'*.
- ✓ Thank everyone for their participation and state that the meeting is formally over.
- ✓ Ask for feedback one-to-one after the call.

## Conference call exercise

1. Review the tips above and pull out those that you and your teams could improve upon.
2. Prioritise your list – which makes the biggest difference? Implement those immediately.
3. Gather feedback in the form of a Feedback Sandwich from participants, the team and yourself, and then you can continually improve on the rest over time.

If you don't master the art of engaging conference calls you'll be contributing to boring calls that don't inspire anyone, but by putting in that extra effort to prepare in advance, you'll be able to run some of the best conference calls in your organisation and business results will be sure to follow.

Now let's take a short interlude to look at the last of the 'Success Stories' and keep an eye out for Ivan's improvements around engagement especially.

## *Success Story – Ivan Information*

*Ivan is a brilliant engineer who loves to understand how things work and fix things that don't. He's worked his way up from apprentice to Director of Engineering and he knows what's what.*

*A new CEO was brought in, and whilst Ivan respected him, he knew he was going to be pushed harder than ever before to do things he really didn't like, or think he was any good at. He was being asked to present at all company meetings and speak up more in the monthly board meeting too.*

*Ivan had given several presentations before he worked with Simply Amazing Training but, whilst he was OK about them, he was always worried that people would ask him a question he didn't know the answer to. He also had more than an inkling that people found his style rather dry and boring. On top of that, the boss said he wanted him to communicate at a more strategic level at the board meeting, but Ivan wasn't sure how* to do that. Ivan's style order is **Information, Caring, Results**, with **Sociable** last.

When we worked together, we started by taking a look at what his monkeys might be. Long story short turns out he had a Red 'You're Wrong' Monkey and an Amber 'You're Boring' Monkey.

The 'You're Wrong' Monkey tracked way back to when he was in English at 7 years old, and he had to spell a word out on the board. He got the spelling wrong by one letter and the teacher said it was wrong. This may not seem like a big deal, but it was to Ivan who, up until then, had been 'teacher's pet' so to speak and able to answer all the class questions. He was actually clever and therefore didn't really know what it felt like to be wrong! From that moment on, his monkey was born to protect him and make sure he was never wrong again. So how would the monkey do that in a presentation? Well the monkey made him read from the slides to ensure he wouldn't 'get it wrong'. The over-worry, about being asked a question he didn't know the answer to, was also in response to not wanting to appear wrong in front of an audience.

The 'You're Boring' Monkey was an Amber Monkey meaning some of it was an over-worry and some of it was true. He didn't make much effort to make his presentations engaging. They were full of facts, with no story or colour, so they were dry. BUT he also worried about being boring based on his experience in the playground when he was younger. The cool kids didn't include him in the gang and he was almost one of the geeky ones, and from then on, he felt he was boring. We 'Tamed' the Amber Monkey and were left with the Green Monkey that it would be beneficial to add some light and shade into his *presentations, especially as they were largely quite technical and data-driven.*

*So, after taming his monkeys we got to work on learning the skills and tools needed to succeed.*

*We went through the SAS, and he was pleased he could have a structure to follow that would result in an organised presentation. He began to see how his presentations in the past had not been 'audience focussed' and were mostly 'push' not 'pull' presentations.*

- *Ivan found the new approach to the Q&T section enlightening. He could prepare for the questions but not in an obsessive manner. He learnt how to manage if he really didn't know the answer, and how to be in the appropriate calm, clear and concise mindset that will, more than often not, mean that he can, in fact, answer the question perfectly well with his current knowledge.*

- *The other thing he learnt was how to bring colour and life to his presentations. Ivan was never going to be an entertainer, and nor did he need to be. But something needed to improve to help him get his message across at the whole company meetings in a more engaging manner. Ivan learnt to tell the story behind the facts and figures and this meant people at all levels could understand his message. He learnt visualisation skills, to make numbers into charts and graphs that were more engaging and more easily understood. He cleaned up his PowerPoint slides too. They went from streams of data to simple graphics explaining one point at a time, meaning he no longer read them word for word.*

- *He loved the idea of strategic thinking. It didn't come naturally, but he knows it's an ongoing area for development. His presentations to the board are already getting better results, and last month, he made his argument so clearly that they agreed with his recommendation and signed off a 150K piece of new kit.*

The CEO was delighted with Ivan's improvements and his new-found confidence at the monthly board meeting. His input and clarity are now greatly appreciated. When he presented his latest project at the whole company meeting, Ivan knew he had come a long way, because people from the factory floor began to engage in conversation about his projects and suggest improvements that could be made from their point of view. That had never happened before.

# Chapter 12
# Advanced techniques and a final word on High Performance Presentations

By now I'm sure you've picked up some helpful ideas around presentation and communication mindsets, tools and skillsets, haven't you? Most of what you need to give consistently engaging, persuasive and inspiring presentations has been covered in this book. Whatever your current level, having this information will help you assess your presentation performance, adapt and improve.

If you only use 10% of what is in this book, you'll be way above the low bar of other people's presentations! If you use 10% and improve upon it each time you present, you'll be well on the way to delivering engaging, persuasive and inspiring presentations. If you only use 20%-30% of what's in this book, and improve upon that each time you'll be well on the way to delivering High Performance Presentations every time.

Before we finish, I wanted to share a few advanced techniques you can use once you have mastered everything else. Skip this section if you aren't ready for it, and go straight to the section 'Moving Forward'. If you are up for it and want more mindsets, skillsets and toolsets – read on!

## *Advanced techniques*

There is so much more I could share but I've forced myself to prioritise my top three Advanced techniques I believe will benefit you the most in your personal development, team management and business life.

- Strategic Thinking - how to consider not just the impact of the decision or recommendation you are making, but also the implications that will have on other areas and across different timescales and in various contexts. (**All styles** especially **Information** & **Caring**).
- Overcoming objections and 'awkward' questions - why people ask difficult questions and the 5 steps that will help you answer these questions more easily
- Advanced Engagement, Persuasion and Inspiration Techniques – you know using tag questions can increase engagement because they make you nod. Don't they? I'll also cover how positive positioning inspires audiences and framing your message appropriately greatly increases levels of persuasion. (**All Styles**).

## Strategic Thinking

There are plenty of books on strategic thinking and many different definitions – these are useful for **all Presenter Personality Styles** who want to achieve more and may be particularly useful for anyone who tends to do things in the detail and struggles to see the bigger picture (**Information** and **Caring**).

As you begin to prepare and fine tune your SAS, make sure you are thinking strategically, especially if the audience is higher level, such as senior management teams, shareholders, boards and executives.

## Three tips to strategic thinking for presentations

### *Tip 1 – Thinking beyond*

Think beyond just you. All too often managers I work with have previously formulated their presentations in a silo, with too little consideration of the impact of their recommendations on the bigger and broader picture, other divisions, departments or interested parties, both now and in the future. There may only be one blind spot, but that can be important. Here are some real-life examples I've seen:

The marketer who worked on a project for 7 months, unaware that the capital investment amount required to make the project happen was never going to be an achievable ask.

The website entrepreneur, who'd developed amazing content and tested it over several years, but hadn't considered how he would communicate the idea and marketing message succinctly to customers.

The doctor bidding for funding who didn't consider how to demonstrate return on investment to the panel.

By using the SAS structure thoroughly, and also consulting with others, you will more than likely catch all reasonable points that might come up in a project meeting or presentation and you can then prepare and adapt your plans accordingly.

Think beyond right now. This may sound a bit grand, but it is critical to motivating the audience and gaining buy-in. This is what Martin Luther King did so well in his *'I have a dream'* speech. You don't have to be a motivational speaker to do this. You need to just share your vision with the audience. Describe what you can see in this new future, what you can hear, what it feels like and ideally how it works.

For example, let's say you want to implement a new CRM (customer relationship management) system. This may not sound very dynamic to begin with – but actually given some thought, it is. A critical part of the SAS in the WHAT section will be to paint a picture of the future with this new system. Use the see, hear, feel formula below:

**See:** with the new system we'll look around the office and see happy customer service representatives, because they can easily input new call information and retrieve previous customer conversations. The satisfaction scores will go up to 90% and call times will decrease by an average of 5 seconds.

**Hear:** we'll hear calmer and shorter customer service calls as issues will be resolved more easily, because the required information is at our teams' fingertips. We'll hear people talking at the coffee machine about how much better this new system is.

**Feel:** the department will feel calmer with fewer customer issues needing to be escalated. Representatives will feel they are able to achieve their targets, and so will feel more motivated, leading to improved staff retention over time.

A note to **Sociable** types: whilst this is often a strength – don't take the picture painting too far. Give the feeling, but keep it on the brief side and don't over-exaggerate.

For **Information**, **Caring** and **Results** types particularly: when you are inspiring a group of people, it is important to show them what the future will look like.

## Tip 2 – Bring solutions not problems

If you bring solutions or a number of options to the table, instead of just problems, you will be demonstrating your ability to think strategically. It will suggest to the senior team that you are capable of dealing with problems that arise.

Scenario planning is thinking about as many possible WHAT IFs and then planning for those. In the implementation of a CRM system, for example, we may want to look at the impacts of:

- Key people leaving during project implementation.
- Unforeseen costs of the project (e.g. making terminals multi-screen to actualise the time-saving benefits).

- A need to expand the system into the accounts department.

It may well be more complicated than that – these are some simple examples to open up your thinking.

Give options, choices and risks when presenting to higher levels. I'd advise against the approach of *'don't mention it and they'll never know'*.

---

**Sociable**

Your strength is creating new ways to think about things – mind you don't bombard others with too many 'part-baked' ideas if it isn't the appropriate forum. Narrow your solutions down to the top few with a recommendation. Ensure your solutions are backed up with the detail, data and facts, and have been looked at from all angles. Don't underplay the risks.

---

**Caring**

You may prefer to come to a consensus decision and involve everyone's views, which is sometimes good for buy-in, but beware because this can look, to other preference styles, like you don't have an opinion or solution and are just waiting for others to think or decide for you. Ensure your proposals are backed up with the detail, data and facts.

> *Information*
>
> You can be relied on to bring all the relevant data with thought-through solutions. Watch out for overloading other preference styles with too much information. You can keep the spare details and ideas in your back pocket in case you need them – hidden slides are great for this. Make sure your solutions consider the people element too. Don't over play the risks.

> *Results*
>
> Be aware that your proposal is not the only option. This should not be a win or lose negotiation. Ensure your solutions consider the people element too and paces the audience appropriately. Even if your idea isn't adopted, it may well start a discussion that does find an acceptable solution, and it certainly shows initiative.

### *Tip 3 – Less is more*

When you are presenting more strategic ideas or projects, less is often more. (**Information, Caring** and **Sociable** preferences take note here.) How much information you need to go into, about how the product or software works, will depend on who you are presenting to and what their interests are.

If you are talking to the technical people who need to know the details, then of course go into the specifics. If, however, you are talking to the board or people who don't need to know (they just want to know that it will work) it is best to share minimal information to help them see how it works and then stop. You can always offer to share more at another stage, and if they want more, they have the opportunity to ask for it in the 'WHAT IF' section.

Generally, the more information you give the more there is to disagree with, and the meeting (and your project) could be side-tracked if you aren't careful. Those with a **Results** preference should take care not to give too little information. Remember the preference types in your audience and adapt your style appropriately.

## You can be too strategic!

Being too strategic isn't a common issue, but it can happen. This will depend on the audience – sometimes senior managers spend so long being strategic, and being around other strategic people, they lose track of the real world. This is why TV reality shows like 'Undercover Boss' are popular – because you get to see strategic people begin to grasp the grass roots issues.

If you run a pizza chain and your staff on the ground can't make good quality pizzas consistently, within cost constraints, then an expensive conference launching the latest marketing strap line, 'Passion, People, Pizza' could be a huge waste of money! People at the coal face generally need to have their everyday issues listened to, and ideally addressed, before they can appreciate big picture or longer-term ideas.

### *Tactical moves*

There is a role for tactical moves, and if this is the content of the presentation then it is good to make that known. This is about introducing your presentation effectively, so people can listen and benefit from the content.

For example, in the LITTLE INTRO you might say, *'This is a tactical plan to address the competitive move by company x'*. Or you might need to justify it, within the WHAT section of the presentation, and reveal within the story that a tactical approach is required. It is important to consider where this fits in with the company's long-term strategy and if it does not, you might want to be open and honest about it, giving others the full information on which to make decisions.

### *Wrap up*

Without strategic thinking skills you could miss the interconnectedness of things, be setting a poor example to your team and unknowingly make poor recommendations for the company as a whole.

Developing strategic thinking skills is a significantly benefit – you'll illustrate your ability to see the bigger picture, to represent the best interest of the company as a whole and thus demonstrate your suitability for bigger projects and more responsibility.

## Overcoming objections and 'awkward' questions

Strangely enough, often when people ask questions, they don't come out with the question they really want answered. We do this naturally – we don't mean to do it! By using this technique I'm about to share you'll:

- ☐ Get to the heart of the matter more quickly.
- ☐ Overcome problems, challenges or objections easily.
- ☐ Demonstrate your strategic thinking.

Questions should be seen as the most amazing opportunity for you to break down any objections or obstacles in the way of the audience going ahead and doing the action you want them to do. Questions, and the way in which you answer them, can be the icing on the SAS cake! All too often though, they are at best a missed opportunity, and at worst a bun fight!

Let's look at some 'awkward' questions that have actually been asked in various situations:

- Factory manager at a board meeting for a new product asked, *'Why do you think sales will increase when they fell last quarter?'*
- Prospective client at a sales pitch, *'Why did you say 25% when the most recent figures actually state 27%?'*
- HR manager asked an interview candidate, *'Why did you make an error on your CV?'*

You may have experienced questions similar to these, and I want to share 5 steps that will help you answer these awkward questions more easily. Whilst these may not seem fast and easy to begin with, as you practise it becomes second nature. In order to illustrate these 5 steps, we'll use the example of the 'awkward' question asked by the factory manager at the board meeting throughout: when discussing a new product, he asked, *'Why do you think sales will increase when they fell last quarter?'*

## Step 1 Assume a positive intention

Before you begin to answer any question, know that there are some mindsets that are useful to have when it comes to developing your advanced communication skills. One of these is to hold in your mind that every behaviour (no matter how destructive or negative it may seem on the surface) has a positive intention for that person or others. It is much nicer and easier to manage any 'awkward' questions or audience behaviours when you start with that mindset. (It may or may not be actually true, but if you act as if it is true, then communicating effectively becomes easier.)

Begin with the belief that all Questions and Thoughts are good and useful. (If you currently have any 'unreasonable' thoughts that the audience are trying to put you down or attacking you, then there is probably a Public Speaking Monkey that needs to be 'Tamed' before you start this process.)

*Factory manager example Step 1:*

*My mindset is that it is good to hear from the factory manager, as he is the one in charge of producing these widgets efficiently and on time.*

## Step 2 Listen and observe fully

Before answering any questions, always listen to the original question properly and observe i.e. be aware of everything about the person. What do you know about them from previous interactions? What Presenter Personality Style preferences do they have? Do they tend to look for the problems or the solutions? Are they big picture or detailed? (This is about reasonable, and possibly unconscious, observations of their Presenter Personality Style, rather than how they feel about you. If you find these questions all coming back to how they feel about you i.e. *'They don't like me'*, then look out, there might be a Public Speaking Monkey about.)

When they asked the question, what did their tonality and body language suggest? Concern, disbelief, curiosity or frustration?

*Factory manager example Step 2:*

*His tonality and body language suggest concern, in the level of belief he can have, in the accuracy of the sales forecast. He has an introverted thinking preference (Information) and a tendency to be cautious and pessimistic.*

## Step 3 Empathy and imagination

Imagine yourself in the other person's shoes (or more accurately, inside their head) and speculate or 'mind read' on the positive reasons they might be asking that question. Imagine what it must be like in their job role listening to your presentation; what might their concerns be?

*Factory manager example Step 3:*

*The original question is doubting the forecast numbers and why those numbers were chosen, which is reasonable. And assuming in the presentation you already gave your thoughts on why there will be an increase, it is likely there is something else concerning him behind the original question. For example:*

  a) *He might be asking this question because he needs to plan the factory staffing – the increase in sales might mean he has to train new staff, and so start the recruiting process next week.*

  b) *He might need to buy in some special ingredients or parts that have a long lead time.*

c) He might remember the previous overenthusiastic marketing person, and the resulting £500k of stock rotting away in a warehouse in Stockport!

d) He might have a holiday booked for next quarter when he thought it would be quiet, but now it is going to be the busiest time of the year.

## Step 4 Predict questions 'behind' the questions

Predict if there might be further, more specific question(s) that are 'behind' the original question. If you feel you have already given a reasonable account of your course of action in the presentation, then it is very likely there is an unsaid and unknown question behind the originally asked question. This is not because anyone is trying to be awkward or hide their thoughts from you, but it seems to be inherent in our language that we ask a different, (perhaps the easier to think of question) but if we chunk up or down enough, then the actual question 'behind' the question is revealed.

*Factory manager example Step 4:*

*'Mind read' what the factory manager's question 'behind' the question could be:*

a) Are we prepared to commit to recruiting new staff next week?

b) Are we prepared to commit to purchasing x by y time?

c) How can we reduce the chances of being left with surplus stock?

d) How will we successfully deliver what you need whilst

*I'm on holiday?*

## Step 5 Clarification

By helping the person asking the question to actually get to their behind question, you'll be demonstrating empathy and that you want to understand their concerns. Instead of reaching a stalemate, you'll decrease friction and enable the business to get to a better and/or faster solution to issues.

Check your mind-reading skills with the person, and if you were correct, answer that more accurate question 'behind' the question instead. Awareness of this demonstrates deep understanding of both your subject and your audience.

*Factory manager example step 5:*

*Check in with the person as to why they were asking the original question. You want to understand why they asked the original question to discover if they were (unconsciously) actually wanting to ask the 'question behind the question'.*

Q: 'Why do you think sales will increase when they fell last quarter?'

- a) 'There are several reasons which I'm happy to go through and, before I do that, can I check ... are you asking because you are concerned about staffing up in time or some other reason?'

- b) 'Before I answer, I want to just check if you are asking because you are thinking about resource planning in the remaining time or something else?'

- c) 'Are you asking that because you are wondering how

we can avoid having excess stock, or for another reason?'

d) 'Are you wondering how the factory will manage such a busy period, or is there something else you are thinking of specifically?'

Let's just take a moment to compare the responses above to the to the potential responses to the original question ...

Original question: 'Why do you think sales will increase when they fell last quarter?'

Potential answers to the original question:

    a. 'Because I've researched all the latest trends and analysed the last 5 years of data.'
    b. 'Because I spoke to the buyers and they assured me they would place an order.'
    c. 'Because I've been doing this for years and I have a great feeling about this.'
    d. 'Because the weather forecast for this quarter is 2.5 degrees warmer.'

Assuming a certain degree of intelligence in the room – you can see the quality of thought has improved dramatically when you check for the question behind. The likelihood of getting into a no-win, chest beating situation is significantly reduced. And your credibility and ability to demonstrate depth of understanding has rocketed, enabling the business to address any risks, concerns or issues. These advanced techniques are worth practising, once you've got the basics right to demonstrate your deep understanding and strategic thinking.

## Advanced Linguistic Techniques

### Advanced Engagement – using tag questions

You already know what a tag question is ... don't you? You might not know it by name, but you've probably heard them used ... haven't you? They are called tag questions because you form a sentence, and then tag a short question onto the end of the initial sentence. That makes sense ... doesn't it?

There are two very commonly used types of tag questions – ones made from positive affirmative sentences, the other made from negative sentences. They are used to demonstrate that you think you know the answer, but when used well, they can do many more things besides. If you use too many at any one time, they can get a little annoying ... can't they?

Tag questions are great for:

**Pacing** – getting confirmation of where the audience is. For example, *'You now know what a tag question is, so I expect you are wondering how you can use them in a* presentation ... aren't you?'

**Building rapport** – if you pace the audience's experience and show you understand them, it helps build rapport. The tag question helps you suggest you know what they are thinking, yet still gives you an opt-out so you don't break rapport.

Read the following two sentences and notice how each one makes you feel different:

*'I expect you are wondering how you'll remember all this when you are doing your next presentation.'*

*'I expect you are wondering how you'll remember all this when you are doing your next presentation ... aren't you?'*

Just adding in the tag question means rapport is maintained with the audience, because it is looking for their input and suggests you are asking, not telling.

**Softening a difficult message** – instead of saying, *'You might find this difficult'* you could say, *'I know when I first started using tag questions it felt a bit awkward to begin with. I didn't always know when the right time to use them was ... You know what I mean ... don't you?'*

In this example, you may want to let the audience know that you understand they may find it difficult. If I was speaking directly, I might have previously said, *'You might find this difficult'* but by being so direct you risk breaking rapport – the audience may become defensive and think to themselves, *'No I won't!'* Instead it is softer to say:

Q: *'This is a little difficult, isn't it? '*

A: *'Yes, it's little difficult. / No, it isn't difficult. / I don't know. '*

And even better, if you've read about the power of positive suggestion, to say:

Q: *'This isn't all that easy, is it?'*

**Empathy** – tag questions in stories can be useful if you want the audience to experience an emotion with you and feel like they have been there too. For example, here are another two sentences to read and see how they make you feel:

*'I was confused, overwhelmed and didn't know what to do.'*

*'I was confused, overwhelmed and didn't know what to do. I'm sure you know what that feels like ... don't you?'*

**Informality** – As a speaker you can use tag questions to your advantage (even if you are 100% sure of the answer) for the purpose of building rapport, engaging the audience and making your talk more conversational.

Example:

*'I'm sure you'd like a quick break now ... wouldn't you?'*

*'You probably want to know how this works in the real world ... don't you?'*

In the audience member's mind, they feel as if you are asking them a question, thus asking their opinion in a way. In their mind or with a nod (if encouraged by the speaker who is also nodding) they will answer you.

With more and more technology comes shorter attention spans, and that is only likely to compound over time. Whether you like it or not, one of the roles of many presentations is to entertain (keep a group of people interested or enjoying themselves) and engage (to interest someone in something and keep them thinking about it). Tag questions help you when used appropriately and sprinkled (not piled) into your presentation.

### Advanced Inspiration Techniques - Positive positioning

If you want people to be inspired and take action then say what you do want, not what you do not want.

The exercise I use in coaching to demonstrate this is in 2 steps:

1. *Close your eyes and do NOT think of a blue tree then open your eyes.*
2. *Notice what you saw in your mind or were thinking of.*

All too often the answer is, 'A blue tree' or, 'A green tree'. But even to get the green tree you had to think of the blue one first, in order to know that's not what you should be thinking about! So, if you want to paint a picture of things you <u>do</u> want in the audience's mind, be careful if you begin to talk about what you <u>don't</u> want. I've heard plenty of presenters say:

*'I hope I don't bore you.'*

*'I hope you don't find this too confusing.'*

*'I hope I don't mess this up.'*

I've got a little rescue dog and we use positive dog training methods for this same reason. If the dog is chewing something and you say 'no', all she knows is she's being told off. She might even stop at that moment, but she doesn't know what she should be doing instead. Positive training is all about enforcing positive behaviour, so if she is found playing with a toy she is told 'yes' and rewarded for her good behaviour.

If you want to inspire people into action (probably in the HOW) tell them what you do want them to do – give them clear positive instructions. Combine that with engaging stories (perhaps in the WHAT 3) of what the future looks like then you'll be onto a winner.

Certainly in the UK this is rarely the way we were brought up (let alone our dogs) so it may take some practice ... say what you would like to see!

Note: Those who have paid close attention so far you will notice in the WHAT IF we do say what we don't want! That is brief and purposeful to motivate those that are motivated by 'away from' language. But it is short and finishes off with an inspirational vision of what we do want.

## Advanced Persuasion - Framing and pre-framing

Framing is the context in which messages are presented. In an experiment quoted from the book, 'Thinking, Fast and Slow' by Daniel Kahneman, subjects were asked whether they would opt for surgery if the 'survival' rate is 90%, while others were told that the 'mortality' rate is 10%. The first framing increased acceptance, even though the situation was no different.

In my experience, people don't spend as long as they could on thinking about how the information or choices are framed. In the experiment, clearly the positive frame rather than the negative worked better, i.e. telling people what they do want to hear, rather than what they do not want to hear. Generally saying what you do want to happen is a good approach to communications. (Having said this, when it comes to motivating people in the WHY section of the SAS, you'll see that a negative motivation can be favourable.)

Pre-framing is setting up the 'frame' for the listener before they even get there. It's like setting up a diversion route to a roadblock ahead of time, so if they get to a certain point they are steered along the new route. (See my use of a simile to explain complex ideas.)

The audience will bring some preconceived ideas with them to the meeting or presentation. For example, they may believe it is going to be boring like it was last year, or they think they already know all about this topic, so why waste their time listening? There are many ways you can overcome these in your presentation by pre-framing the potential objection.

If you think they will have the 'already know it so I don't need to listen' syndrome, you can address it in advance, almost beating them to it in a way. You can put a different angle on their pre-existing attitude, for example:

*'Some of you may have heard this or similar things before, which is great, but the question is, are you implementing the knowledge in all parts of the business every day? If not, this will help you to see new areas and new ways to ...'*

or

*'For those of you who've heard me talk about this before and who have implemented the new system, thanks! We'd now love you to play a mentoring role in the organisation helping others implement the changes, so refreshing on some key points means you'll be able to answer any questions from colleagues.'*

Of course, you know what will work in your organisation, but the idea is to acknowledge that they may come in with a specific, less helpful attitude, and then plan some appropriate words to neutralise that objection. You might even include a relevant and surprising question or fact, which may help them see they actually don't know it all.

## *Moving forward*

If you have an important communication or presentation, you know better than to just open up the laptop and start typing up slides or choosing fonts! Instead, grab a pen and paper and scope it all out before you touch the computer.

Next time, get to planning your SAS as soon as you hear about the presentation. It can be a very quick process (especially once you are practised at it) and it will help you to feel calm and relaxed as you know (big picture) what you are going to say.

Having asked your unconscious mind to pay attention to the task, in advance of the presentation, will help you to feel confident that it is in hand; your unconscious mind will be coming up with good ideas, potential concerns and so on, all in good time to create a High Performance Presentation.

I know what some of you are thinking: it all moves so quickly around here, you don't want to write your presentation too early because things would have changed – you need to include the latest figures, customer needs, research findings. The good news is you can still do the SAS early, and then leave the presentation creation to nearer the time. The details and specifics can be added once you've worked on the framework, and of course, the creation of visuals (if you do need PowerPoint for example) becomes so much faster when you know what you want to say. Instead of lots of words, just a few key images, points and perhaps graphs are great.

Begin to get to the point where you can say you use the SAS

technique every time you have an important presentation. Run your rough structure past colleagues to ask for feedback and make it better and better.

Learn your content in the easy manner laid out in the book, so you can be comfortable with your flow, speak easily from the heart and make eye contact with the audience.

Practise your presentation using your preparation time wisely. Instead of wasting time practising bits you already know, get efficient with your precious practice time, and make the most of it.

When you present, always review your progress (using the Feedback Sandwich). Feedback on yourself and your teams — did you inspire action or did the audience consequently do nothing differently from before? Had you anticipated all the objections you received? Did you cover everything you needed to for all of the people in the room, including risks, costs, timings, projections etc? High Performance Presentations require focus of effort, attention to really do the job well and a commitment to improve.

## Presenter Styles Summary

Throughout this book we've looked at understanding your own style, the styles of your audience, and bridging the gap so your communication is effective and useful to all.

No matter what your style, play to your strengths and minimise your weaknesses. The best thing is to be flexible in all Presenter Personality Styles — no matter what your preference, to be able to flex style to suit audience and context — and also to allow yourself to contribute with the things that make you unique.

There will always be exceptions to rules. We can generalise Presenter Personality Styles, but if you are very much one style and you make that your unique brand, it will work. If you have a quirk, you can choose to make the most of it. Now that you know the rules, you can decide when to follow them and where you want to break them.

> **Be natural, engaging and let your personality shine through**

## Nobody's perfect

If things go wrong, you now have the information to understand and reflect on what happened and do things differently next time. And if things go 'OK', pick areas in this book, one at a time, where you or your teams can improve even further. Remember, average presentations bring average results (at best).

Despite teaching this, even I can't say I implement all of it 100% of the time! But I do know when I've not implemented it! I know when a talk or presentation didn't go as well as I wanted it to (even though others haven't consciously noticed it). I might feel that I didn't make it as easy as I could have for the audience to understand a key message, or I notice that I could have been stronger in inspiring action or wrapped up more effectively.

And whilst it maybe hasn't damaged my business that one time, I'm aware that longer term, if I never corrected myself, it would.

When you start to practise the mindsets, toolsets and skillsets in this book, even just one at a time, you'll notice your presentations come on in leaps and bounds. People, at all levels in the organisation, will start to notice you and your unique and effective presentation style.

No matter what level you are, it is always good to improve. The tips in this book are especially valuable on the days when you think you can't create the time to use them. Even 5 minutes of preparation can make a big difference if you use those minutes well.

As you get better and better you'll be asked to do more presentations, chair more meetings and take on more responsibility. When you deliver engaging, persuasive and inspiring presentations every time you'll be impressing other people without even knowing it: customers, suppliers, other industry experts. Just get up there and present with the best intention for the audience in mind, and your confidence, your teams and your career will likely benefit too.

> **Grab all opportunities and get yourself and your team noticed for your skills and abilities. Strive to always prepare and give High Performance Presentations – no doubt it will lead to more success.**

Also by this author:

Taming Your Public Speaking Monkeys
Building Confidence for Public Speaking and Presentations

For other recommended reading please visit:
www.SimplyAmazingTraining.co.uk/Recommended-Reading/

If you have enjoyed

## High Performance Presentations

I'd love it if you'd share it with the people you know – buy them a copy or share the link on social media, or post your review on Amazon.

You can email me at Dee@SimplyAmazingTraining.co.uk, connect with me on LinkedIn or visit our website

www. SimplyAmazingTraining.co.uk

I welcome your feedback.

Happy engaging, persuading and inspiring!

Dee.

Printed in Great Britain
by Amazon